SNOOKER'S BAD BOYS

Matt Bozeat

SNOOKER'S BAD BOYS

The Feuds, Fist Fights and Fixes

pitch

First published by Pitch Publishing, 2023
Reprinted 2025

Pitch Publishing
9 Donnington Park,
85 Birdham Road,
Chichester,
West Sussex,
PO20 7AJ
www.pitchpublishing.co.uk
info@pitchpublishing.co.uk

© 2023, Matt Bozeat

Every effort has been made to trace the copyright.
Any oversight will be rectified in future editions at the
earliest opportunity by the publisher.

All rights reserved. No part of this book may be reproduced,
sold or utilised in any form or transmitted in any form or by
any means, electronic or mechanical, including photocopying,
recording or by any information storage and retrieval system,
without prior permission in writing from the Publisher.

A CIP catalogue record is available for this book
from the British Library.

ISBN 978 1 80150 445 4

Printed and bound in the UK on FSC® certified paper in line
with our continuing commitment to ethical business practices,
sustainability and the environment.

Printed and bound by CPI Antony Rowe, UK

Contents

The Hurricane and Friends 9

'I Hate Steve Davis' 43

'You Can't Buy Youth' 74

Cocaine Kirk and the Canadians 88

The Melter 111

The Class of '92 and the Laughing Latvian . . 132

One Night with The Hurricane 148

'The Rocket' and His Rivals 163

Fights and Fixes 185

Jimmy Brown and the Rest of the Cast 201

Bibliography 205

For Mum, Dad and Carla Diana

THE HURRICANE AND FRIENDS

ON SUNDAY nights, with a return to school or work only a sleep away, there was one way to raise a smile.

Spitting Image hit ITV screens at ten o'clock and for half an hour this very adult puppet show pointed a rubbery finger of ridicule at politicians, sportsmen – anyone who deserved it.

One episode featured a letter that read: 'Why can't there be more snooker on television?

'PS: I am mad.'

This was at a time when it was estimated there was more than 80 days' coverage of snooker on the major television channels – and it was popular with viewers.

Only soap opera *Coronation Street* and comedians Morecambe and Wise kept snooker off the top of the television ratings and in July 1987, the *New York Times* described snooker as 'by far the most widely watched sport in Britain'.

Steve Davis explained the appeal. He said: 'It was new on TV. Once they started showing it as a storyline it sucked people into the rest of it. We had a trapped audience.

'No Sunday shopping, nowhere near as many people going out for meals, no internet, no PlayStation. People watched television quite a lot more.'

Until November 1982 there were only three television channels to choose from and viewers had to get off the sofa to change channels.

The Sunday trading laws kept shops shut on the Sabbath, when tournaments usually came to a conclusion, and faced with a choice between an old movie, soap opera and snooker on Sunday afternoons, millions chose snooker.

SNOOKER WAS first seen on television in 1937 when Sydney Lee gave a demonstration at the BBC's studios in Alexandra Palace and later that year, a match between Horace Lindrum and Willie Smith was screened.

The *Radio Times* wrote around that time that over the previous five years, there had been a shift from billiards to snooker in the public's affections.

The feature read: 'It was the custom of the well-known professionals to play an occasional game of snooker after a long session of billiards.

'The game was seldom contested in a really serious spirit, and it seemed merely to act as a sedative after the tenseness of the game that had gone before. Frequently half the onlookers would file out of the hall when the marker announced a snooker match would be played.

'A visit to your local club or hall would have revealed that nine out of every ten tables were devoted to billiards. There was a professional snooker championship, but it was soon over and attracted comparatively little attention.'

The turning point in snooker's fortunes was said to be the introduction of a national amateur competition run on a handicap basis, in 1933. The feature continued: 'To the surprise of everybody concerned, especially the organisers, there was an entry of no fewer than 5,000, which brought the realisation that snooker had begun to take root.'

Professional snooker still struggled, the writer observing it was 'a periodic game ... Without the aid of frequent matches between the well-known players it was impossible to popularise snooker and the game was almost at a standstill until a year or two later when the necessary impetus came in a most unexpected fashion.

'A certain amount of publicity attended the visit to this country of the famous Canadian snooker player, Conrad Stanbury.

'Stanbury was above all a colourful player and as such was a godsend, in that his personality drew attention to the game. In the matter of breaks he was not as good as our own Joe Davis, but his unique strokeplay was all that was necessary to bring in spectators.'

DAVIS WAS born in Whitwell, Derbyshire in April 1901 and learned to play billiards at his family's pub, the Queen's Hotel in Whittington Moor, where he would play before school, during lunch breaks and after school.

His billiards education included coaching sessions with Ernest Rudge in the billiard room he had built at the bottom of his garden, along with hours spent studying Charles Dawson's *Practical Billiards* book. The work paid off and aged 12, Joe made his first century.

Davis took more interest in snooker after taking over the management of a billiard hall in Chesterfield. Although initially unwilling to embrace a sport that he referred to as 'slapdash' in a newspaper article, Davis noticed snooker becoming more popular with his customers.

A pair of billiard traders, George Nelson from Leeds and Bill Camkin from Birmingham, also recognised snooker's possibilities and with their backing, Joe asked the sport's governing body to give their support to the first World Snooker Championship.

Davis won the inaugural event in 1927 – even though he couldn't see properly. He had a lazy right eye, meaning he had to rest his cue on the left-hand side of his chin and line up shots with his left eye.

Encouraged by his world title success, Davis set about raising snooker's standards. Tom Newman's break of 89 in 1919 had stood as snooker's highest recorded break for six years until Davis bettered it with a 96 and by 1933, Davis had raised that to 114, changing the way snooker was played by building breaks around the black ball.

Walter Lindrum, the Australian who had proved to be Davis's master at billiards, was beaten on the snooker table and another challenger came from the same family …

Horace Lindrum, a nephew of Walter, had a vociferous backer in mother Clara, and in 1934 she took her chance to set up a challenge match with Davis.

Joe had lost the World Billiards Championship Final to Walter Lindrum in Australia and was set to return home when Clara challenged him to a snooker match on her son Horace's behalf, saying Davis was 'a phoney' and that even she could beat him.

Davis slapped down a £300 stake that she matched and in front of sell-out crowds in Melbourne, Joe confirmed he was the world's No. 1 with a 42-22 win.

Horace was more competitive in the World Snooker Championship Final in 1936 and edged ahead 27-24. Davis responded by winning the next ten frames to retain the title and for good measure, he went on to beat Lindrum in the next year's final as well.

Another challenge to Joe's snooker dominance came from his own family.

Joe beat younger brother Fred in the semi-finals in 1939 and in the following year's final, sealed a nail-biting 37-35 win with a break of 101.

Davis found another rival in the North East of England.

THE FIRST 'People's Champion' of cue sports was born in Darlington in January 1886.

Willie Smith would say 'working classes' or the 'average chap' were his biggest supporters.

He played billiards and snooker at a fast pace, had spats with his rivals and took his exhibitions to the country's working men's clubs at a time when most were held at exclusive clubs in London.

But he got it wrong when he claimed the public would never warm to snooker the way they warmed to billiards.

Both sports were a pastime of the elite – to have a table at home was a sign of wealth – and those at the opposite end of the social spectrum who gambled and hustled in smoky taverns and clubs.

The 1969 *Personna Year Book of Sports* referred to the practice of what was known as 'giving a mug a game' in billiard halls during the 1930s.

The book said talented cuemen would 'take on a stranger, assessing his skill, letting him win a good lead, then offer to play for a side bet and the cost of the table hire.

'The stranger usually had a fair run for his money, but if he happened to win, there was liable to be a rough-house between him and the loser's mates. But many a man learned to play billiards this hard way.'

The roots of snooker and billiards are found in the French aristocracy.

Louis XI of France is believed to be the first to have taken balls off the lawn and on to the table in the 15th century, but snooker as we know it first took shape around 400 years later.

In 1875, Sir Neville Chamberlain was an officer in the British Army based in India and would spend rainy afternoons playing variations of billiards, including pyramids, a game which had a pack of 15 reds.

Chamberlain said it was his idea to add more coloured balls and he stumbled upon a name for this new game after a conversation with a fellow officer.

He used the term 'snooker' to describe a first-year cadet lacking in military know-how and after one of his colleagues missed a simple pot, Chamberlain called him, jokingly, 'a snooker'.

To save his friend's embarrassment, Chamberlain decided every one of his group was 'a snooker' because they were all new to the game and quite hopeless at it.

Stories of snooker reached England and billiards champion John Roberts met Chamberlain in India, found out about the new game and took the rules home with him.

It would take time for snooker to replace billiards in the public's affections and Smith became a star of billiards when he handed Australian George Gray a rare defeat in a billiards match in Stockton in 1911.

The press reported it was Gray's first defeat in England, a fact that would have surprised Smith.

He said Gray was 'not a billiards player at all' after beating him.

Smith did things his way. Clive Everton, the esteemed journalist and commentator, wrote that Smith had little regard for the establishment after the billiards authorities declared him a professional at 15, having discovered he accepted expenses for playing at Middlesbrough Conservative Club.

Smith also played the game his way, as Stanley Newman, who twice reached the last four of the World Snooker Championship, recognised in his book *How to Play Snooker*.

Newman observed that Smith 'is the only player in the front rank that cues two or three inches away from the cue ball. That is to say, when he is addressing the ball, the tip of the cue is a ball or more away from the cue ball on the stroke. That is a very unusual idiosyncrasy, but in Smith's case, effective.

'But Willie Smith is a law unto himself, everybody in the world of professional billiards and snooker realises.'

Smith started playing cue sports after his parents took over running the Golden Cock pub in Darlington when he was a boy. Legend has it, Smith was hustling drinkers by the age of ten and he won the World Billiards Championship in 1920.

Melbourne Inman had won the championship six times previously (1908, 1909, 1912, 1913, 1914 and 1919), but in 1920 he didn't enter and was there when Smith won the title to remind him he was 'the undefeated champion'.

Smith retorted, 'Of course you are. If you don't enter, you can't be beaten.'

That was followed by an exchange of views that ended with the players arranging a money match at Thurston's.

From Twickenham, north London, Inman was a character who knew how to get under the skin of his opponents.

He was an aggressive competitor and in the rather more patient and measured Tom Reece, he found a rival.

Reece, previously a promising swimmer, spent five weeks between 3 June and 6 July 1907 compiling a world record break of 499,135. He played an astonishing 249,522 consecutive cannons and there were stories that W. Chapman, his opponent, left days, possibly weeks, before Reece finished his marathon at Burroughes and Watts club in Soho Square.

The public couldn't bear to watch either.

Reece remembered, 'I generally used to play until the audience had gone. One day, though, a fellow played me a dirty trick. He got in the far corner of the room and I went on making hundred after hundred and kept having a look at him, but he never offered to go. At last I felt too tired to go on and so put my cue down and as he still did not move I went and had a look at him. I found him fast asleep.'

Three times Reece met Inman in the final of the World Billiards Championship (1912–14) and each time, Inman won, benefitting from several flukes along the way.

'How did you do that?' asked Reece after he was on the receiving end.

Inman answered, 'I believe you know my terms for tuition, Mr Reece.'

Such exchanges were common during their matches and after them as well.

Following the 1919 final, Lord Alverston, president of the Billiards Association, was about to present Inman with the trophy, days after sentencing Dr Crippen to death for murdering his wife.

Reece piped up: 'Excuse me, My Lord, but if you knew as much as I do about Inman, you would have given Crippen the cup and sentenced Inman to death.'

Inman often upset those he shared a road with as well. He was known as an erratic driver and on one occasion, Inman was driving home from an exhibition and mowed down a row of red lamps.

The nightwatchman went to confront Inman and Inman said, 'I've taken all the reds, where are the bloody colours?'

The possibility of a match between Inman and Smith created huge interest. The public wanted to know whether the current champion or the undefeated champion who preceded him was No. 1 – and they wanted to bet on the outcome as well.

The match was played at Thurston's and they took £1,800, a huge amount for the time.

Inman started as the 11/10 favourite and took a 1,000-point lead – because Smith allowed him to.

Once Smith's supporters had all placed their bets, he started to play to his best and ran out a convincing winner.

This was common in money matches at the time.

The thrashing of Inman made Smith the No. 1 in the eyes of the public, but he chose not to defend his title in 1921.

He felt the championship should be moved to a larger venue. Thurston's only had room for 172 spectators and Smith wanted to fill more seats, more affordably priced for his supporters.

Smith also knew he could make more money playing exhibitions and arranging money matches on his own terms.

Perhaps the greatest rewards would be in a match against his successor as world champion.

Tom Newman was crowned world champion in 1921 in Smith's absence and the public wanted to see them meet to determine the true No. 1.

Smith and Newman faced each other in a series of matches held over a week and presumably both earned well from them.

The one player Smith couldn't beat was Walter Lindrum, who could compile points twice as quickly as Smith using close cannons, nudging his cue ball off the other two for hour after hour.

Smith drifted away from competitions, became embittered and had spats with several players, including Joe Davis.

Davis beat him when they met on the billiards table and the outcome was the same when they met in the final of the World Snooker Championship in both 1933 and 1935. Davis and Smith became friends and in January 1955, Davis made the first recorded 147 against Smith at Leicester Square Hall.

Smith lived to be 96 years old and never changed his opinion of snooker. Two years before his death in 1982 he was asked about the sport and said, 'They should change the rules – all of them.'

Smith had played exhibitions into his seventies and entertained audiences with stories from his colourful past.

He remembered an exhibition tour with a player called Diggle, who was convinced he was being followed.

Diggle always kept a gun by the side of his bed and one night, Smith was woken by Diggle shouting, 'They're here, Willie, they're here,' and he fired two shots through the bedroom door before going back to sleep.

Smith stopped playing in 1966, giving his cue to a doctor and never striking a ball again.

JOE DAVIS kept winning the World Snooker Championship until 1946, when he retired.

In retirement, he remained snooker's biggest – and most influential – character. As the head of the Professional Billiards Players' Association, Davis effectively ran snooker and when he fancied it and the rewards were there, he would come out of retirement.

He decided who could turn professional and to preserve snooker's image, he kept out colourful rogues like Pat Houlihan and Dickie Laws, who earned their reputations playing in money matches.

Legend has it, Houlihan was once woken by an associate of the Krays and taken to play Tommy Smithson in a money match. Smithson was later murdered in what the press recorded as 'a gangland slaying'.

The Krays had an interest in snooker after buying the Regal Billiard Hall on Eric Street in Mile End in the east end of London in 1954.

John Pearson wrote of the Regal in his book *The Profession of Violence*: 'Most thieves require a well-run base if they can find it, somewhere they can relax, talk freely, pick up the latest gossip and know they are safe. For them, the billiard hall was perfect ...

'Thieves could leave the tools of their trade on the premises; in an emergency the twins might even look after a thief's takings for him ... before long the billiard hall was offering criminals a genuine service.

'It was all carefully organised.

'There were lock-up cubicles under the seats for the thieves' tools, stolen goods could be left round the back of the hall ...

'The billiard hall was a good receiving ground for criminal information, a word from a fence, a tip-off from a taxi driver, a telephone call from a barman.'

In such places, Houlihan made his living.

Jean Rafferty wrote in *The Cruel Game*: 'In the days before television made snooker a game people actually knew about, Pat was a hustler, who travelled all round the country pretending to be a worse player than he was and relieving people of the trouble of having to carry their money around with them.'

Houlihan, from Deptford in south-east London, said: 'What I used to do was walk in, go up to the counter and say: "Cup of tea please and I'll have a roll." And then all I'd do was pull out a few quid and all of a sudden you've got people coming up to you going: "All right? Fancy a game?" And I'd say: "Nah" and I'd sit down and have my tea and then some fella would say: "Anybody else?" and I'd say: "All right, then."

'I'd let them win for not a lot of money and then they're thinking, "This is all right," and then I'd start coming back. Once a fella said to me: "Want two quid on it? I'll give you a 16-point start." I ended up getting £140 off him, which was a lot of money in those days.'

There was no money to be made in professional snooker and anyway, they wouldn't have Houlihan.

His wasn't the image Davis wanted for his sport. 'It was very hard to turn pro,' said Houlihan. 'It was sewn up in them days.

'Joe Davis was kingpin and his word was bond. When he said "Yes" or "No" that was it.'

Such was his approach to snooker, Houlihan was only ever going to hear 'No'.

He looked to make money from snooker when there was no money to be made. 'You can't eat trophies,' he said once and Houlihan had a family to feed.

He knew that sometimes, losing was good for business. One promoter described Houlihan as 'crooked as a donkey's hind leg' after he lost 'deliberately'.

Houlihan would practise missing, but when he played to win, he could be unstoppable. He was recorded making a century in under four minutes and told *The Observer* in 2002: 'I gave them 100-plus starts, played left-handed, one-handed ... I played a fella for money with the bottom of my cue.

'I had the flair. I was very fast.'

Everyone wanted to watch him. 'I was the draw in them days,' said Houlihan. 'I remember once playing in the Burroughes Hall in Soho Square. They had to have two police cars to control the crowds. I couldn't even get myself in. I had to force my way through the crowd. I always got a good living then. If I didn't in London, I went elsewhere.

'Once, someone suggested going to Jersey, but when I got there, I was known. There was nothing for me in Jersey, but I used to have a good life going around. You always ended up in the pub. You'd play snooker in the afternoon and then have a nice drink in the evening.'

Contemporaries remembered Houlihan would drink and seldom eat.

ASKED IN 1959 about the future of professional snooker, Fred Davis replied: 'It has no future.'

At the time there were only a handful of professional players – and most of them didn't need snooker.

Fred got an income from the family farm, Rex Williams had a share in the family's printing business and Jack Rea brought in money as a comedian.

As world champion for 11 years, John Pulman was able to scrape a living from exhibitions, but from 1957 to 1964 he went unchallenged as world champion.

Pulman, a tall, bespectacled Devonian, was a character, as Fred Davis remembered in his book *Talking Snooker*.

He wrote: 'Fiery and temperamental in that his language was inclined to go over the edge if things were not going well ... some spectators found John more entertaining when things were going badly than well because they were more likely to see fireworks.

'He was never slow to show his displeasure at any distraction: a spectator moving, blowing his nose, whispering to a friend or – surely a case for the death penalty – eating a bag of crisps.

'As a young player, he was inclined to be impetuous. Many was the time when, having been 40 or 50 in front with three or four reds left, he would chance a pot with the odds more in favour of fencing for a better opening, only to miss the pot and leave his opponent the opportunity to clear the table. On top of his natural impatience, then, would be the fury and frustration of having lost a frame he knew he should have won.'

Pulman responded: 'I am convinced that [to succeed at snooker] you must have the temperament whereby you will get annoyed with yourself when you are not playing as well as you should.

'The player who gets annoyed with himself will tend to force himself to play better through sheer grit and determination. I am sure that only such a person can be a champion.'

Nobody knew Pulman better than Davis, on the table at least. They contested five World Championship finals. Pulman won three, including the classic 1965 final, played over the best of 73 frames over six days at Burroughes Hall in Soho Square.

At 36-35 behind, Pulman was only one frame from defeat, but he sent the match into a deciding 73rd frame with breaks of 27 and 23.

Davis made the first mistake in the decider, letting Pulman in for a break of 32. Another run of 33 took Pulman 40 points clear and with only four colours remaining, the World Championship was his.

The result barely made any newspaper headlines and didn't make Pulman much money either.

Once he played an impressive shot at an exhibition and someone said: 'He isn't world champion for nothing.'

'Next to nothing,' quipped Pulman instantly.

Pulman was known for his wit.

Up against a slow player, he would say, 'If you played him in a week's match, he'd take a fortnight,' and if Pulman was on the receiving end of a fluke he would say, 'If he tossed up a penny, it'd come down half a crown.'

He put down one opponent by saying: 'The last time he beat me, a star appeared in the East.'

Pulman was also happy to criticise the playing conditions, saying once: 'You need a map from the AA to play on this table.'

No wonder Alex Higgins would sneak into a pub in the Royal Arcade in Belfast when underage whenever Pulman was playing on television and watch.

Television appearances were rare, however.

ITV expressed an interest in snooker in 1961, screening a tournament that brought together four amateurs and four professionals, and three years later, coverage of the Northern final of the English Amateur Championships gave the public their first sight of future world champion John Spencer.

In an attempt to ensure continued television coverage, the amateur sport's governing body encouraged players to ensure matches went to a deciding frame to guarantee excitement and that revelation damaged snooker's credibility and led to the sport disappearing from ITV's schedules.

Joe Davis negotiated with the BBC and they would screen him playing frames against fellow professionals. On other occasions, the balls would be spread invitingly and Davis would be asked to make the biggest break possible in two minutes.

Pulman was once filmed making a century break, but mostly, his talents went unrecognised.

Pulman had come to prominence in snooker circles when winning the English Amateur Championship in 1946 at the first attempt at the age of 22.

That secured the support of Bill Lampard, a baker and confectioner who built a billiard room at his house, where Pulman stayed. The relationship apparently broke down after Lampard found Pulman in bed with his wife.

Pulman was known as a womaniser and drinker and following his divorce in the late 1970s, he was declared bankrupt with debts of £5,916.

He was left living in a hotel and spent six months in hospital after being knocked down by a London bus.

Pulman went on to become a snooker commentator with ITV, but was twice asked to leave the commentary box because he was inebriated!

JIMMY WHITE gave three reasons snooker became so popular.

'Colour television, *Pot Black* and Alex Higgins ...'

Without them, Steve Davis might have been a bank manager.

'I was good at maths at school,' said Davis, 'and my mother had plans for me to work in a bank.'

As for White ...

'A rock star maybe ...' he said. 'I've been a snooker player since I was 13 years old. I don't know how to do anything else.'

The advent of colour television gave Davis and White the chance to change their destinies.

The BBC looked for ways to increase sales of colour televisions and so boost viewing figures for their fledgling channel, BBC Two.

A producer, Philip Lewis, who had previously worked on snooker on *Grandstand*, thought snooker could be an attraction and asked Ted Lowe to come up with a weekly format that would suit television audiences.

Lowe had spent his life in snooker. He had started playing billiards at his aunt's pub, graduated to snooker and a cheeky letter written to Joe Davis led to a meeting with the multiple world champion and a challenge match. Davis was impressed by Lowe and got him a job as the general manager of his Leicester Square Hall snooker club that was regarded as the sport's headquarters.

Lowe's life changed at the 1946 World Snooker Championships. His job was to hand score updates to Raymond Glendenning for him to read out on the radio. Glendenning, however, was unable to do his job one night and the panicking producer pleaded with Lowe to step in. Ted, worried he would disturb his boss playing just a few feet away, whispered the scores to the millions listening and would go on to whisper many more times in his career as a television commentator for the BBC.

'A lot of people will tell you Ted did more for snooker than he's given credit for,' said John Williams, a leading referee on the circuit for 28 years.

Williams remembers there being 'plenty of retired BBC television executives' at Ted's funeral in 2011 and said: 'They were saying Ted used to be on the phone to them every day asking, "When are you going to put a tournament on television?"

'He did as much as anyone to convince the television executives they should show more snooker. The players today don't realise how much they owe to Ted.'

Lowe had ruled that players at Joe Davis's club had to be smartly dressed – 'dark suit during the day and a tuxedo in the evenings' – and insisted on the same for *Pot Black*.

Pot Black was Lowe's answer to Lewis's suggestion that there should be snooker on BBC Two.

Eight players would be split into two round-robin groups of four with each match crucially comprising a single, sudden-death frame to make it more palatable for the general public.

Lowe insisted players were well dressed and the theme music – George Botsford's rinky-dink 'Black and White Rag' – also gave viewers the impression they were about to enter an elite, upmarket gentlemen's club.

Pot Black was first screened on 23 July 1969 and from the start, audiences of between one and two million were sucked in and soothed by the drama.

Matches were pre-recorded and screened later in the year. 'Times have changed,' said Steve Davis. 'These days, the results would be all over the internet before the programme had been shown.'

Davis was 11 when the first *Pot Black* was screened and said: 'I was still at school when I started watching.

'I wasn't playing snooker. But my father would watch it and it was such an important part of snooker's success.

'If you did well in *Pot Black* you could add a nought to your earnings through exhibitions.

'There weren't many tournaments and you would be grafting away all year for two tournaments.

'Do well in *Pot Black* and the phone would start ringing and all of a sudden, being a snooker player becomes a proper job.'

The exhibition circuit was boosted after certain gaming machines were legalised and placed in snooker clubs, providing the owners with more revenue that they could invest in staging exhibitions.

'The power of television cannot be underestimated,' said Davis. 'Without *Pot Black* I don't think we would have gone to the Wimbledon-style coverage of the World Championships that came along.'

Ray Reardon won the inaugural *Pot Black* in 1969 with an 88-29 win over John Spencer in the final.

Reardon said: 'We took it [snooker] into people's homes. People who had never seen a game of snooker.

'It was seen around the world. I was in Australia and a woman said, "You're Ray Reardon." How does she know?'

Graham Miles won it in 1974 – after replacing Fred Davis – and it changed his life.

Fred Davis wrote: 'From having a real struggle, he reached the relative security of being one of snooker's highest earners.

'Sections of the public, particularly women, who previously would not have known a snooker ball from a bar of soap, found snooker, with its civilised atmosphere, a refreshing change from the tantrums and violence one sees in other sports.'

But it was still exciting.

Jimmy White said: 'When I was about 11 and started to find snooker from pool I remember watching Alex Higgins play a shot on *Pot Black*.

'There was a black over the middle pocket and he potted it off two cushions with check side when there was a much easier way to pot it.

'He was a massive influence on me ... you couldn't wait to see what he did next.'

Higgins didn't enjoy the single-frame format and the programme's bosses said he was difficult to work with.

Producer Jim Dumighan said: 'We asked the players where to stand and he was irked by that.

'On one recording night, three young ladies showed up in reception saying they were Alex's guests. They represented a well-known Birmingham escort agency.'

There were stories that Higgins urinated in the sink in his changing room, claiming the toilet was too far away, but Dumighan denied he was ever banned from *Pot Black*, as had been rumoured.

The success of *Pot Black* led to West Nally, a west London business specialising in sports sponsorship, creating Park Drive 2000. It brought together four top professionals to play a triple round robin event with the first- and second-placed players meeting in the final.

The BBC screened the best-of-seven-frames final, John Spencer beating Rex Williams, with Gary Owen and John Pulman the other entrants.

TO THE public, Ray Reardon was what a snooker player should be.

He was a smartly dressed and thoughtful tactician who, win or lose, always had a firm handshake and a kind word for his opponent.

Born in Tredegar, Wales in 1932, Reardon discovered cue sports aged eight when his uncle Dan make a makeshift billiards game on the kitchen table.

Reardon was given a snooker table for Christmas and by the age of ten he was playing at Tredegar Workmen's Institute twice a week.

He followed his father Ben down the pits at 15, wearing white gloves to protect his hands, much to the amusement of his work colleagues.

Pit closures forced the Reardons to relocate to Staffordshire in 1956 in pursuit of work.

Reardon decided on a career change after a mining accident left him trapped for several hours and he joined the Stoke-on-Trent police force in 1960 as a probationary constable.

He was given a commendation for convincing a man with a loaded gun to give himself up and would later say his years in the police force were good preparation for a career in snooker.

'It stood me in good stead,' he said during an interview with Michael Parkinson, watched by millions of Saturday night viewers on BBC One.

'Gave me a cool head, evaluate a situation and get on with it.'

These attributes helped him win six World Championships in the 1970s.

'When I won the world title in 1970 in London,' he remembered, 'while I'm waiting for them to make the presentation, suddenly I became aware of someone standing at my side.

'He didn't say to me, "Well done for achieving your life's ambition." He said: "I'm playing you in three months' time in the North West and I'm going to bump you."'

This was the same Irishman who was rumoured to be walking into clubs in Blackburn saying: 'I'm a snooker player. I play for money. Who'll play me?'

Alex Higgins denied ever saying those words, but it gave him the gunslinger's image his management wanted for him.

John McLoughlin, his first manager, added to the legend. 'He has only three vices,' he said. 'Drinking, gambling and women.'

McLoughlin gave him the nickname 'Hurricane', but Higgins preferred 'Alexander the Great'.

McLoughlin was a bingo promoter in Lancashire, where Higgins headed to further his snooker education.

'When I first met him he was really in a mess,' remembered McLoughlin. 'His clothing was in a shabby state, he had holes in his socks, he was through to the blacking on his socks. He really was in despair.'

But he could play snooker like no one McLoughlin had ever seen.

'They kept coming to me and saying you should see this guy who's wandered into the old post office billiard hall with a cue and a meat pie in his hand, that's all he had,' said Dennis Broderick, a business associate of McLoughlin's.

'I didn't take much notice at first, but when I went down I had never seen anything like it in my life. He was so fast.'

McLoughlin, Broderick and Jack Leeming became Higgins's first managers.

HIGGINS GREW up on Abingdon Street in Belfast without the guiding influence of his father after a lorry hit him and left him with learning difficulties.

His mother and three sisters doted on him and he appeared to develop a loathing for authority after a run-in with a punctual school teacher.

Higgins was proud of the new football strip his mother had bought him, but the first time he wore it at school he was five minutes late for his games lesson and sent back to the changing room.

He found what he was looking for when he poked his head around the door of The Jampot, a snooker club just off Donegall Road in Belfast.

'Kids at that age are daring,' he said. 'They like to do things they aren't allowed to do and, in my case, you weren't allowed to go to the dreaded Jampot.

'In the beginning, that was the attraction.'

Once inside, the 11-year-old Higgins was captivated by the clack of the brightly coloured balls and the characters he could see through the fug of cigarette smoke.

'The tobacco smoke hung thick,' he wrote in his autobiography, *Alex Through the Looking Glass*, 'and the light was so dim it could have been night.'

The gamblers, hustlers and wide boys he saw there inhabited an exciting, dangerous world, living from one turn-of-the-card thrill to the next.

The regulars at The Jampot were glad to see the young Higgins. They thought he would be easy pickings.

'Probably one of the reasons I play the game so fast,' he said years later, 'is because at The Jampot, when you played for no money and got beat, you got a cue over your head.'

But by the age of 12, Higgins was a polished hustler. Fuelled by Coca-Cola and Mars bars, he rushed around the table and he won more matches than he lost.

'As soon as school was over, I would play a solid four hours,' said Higgins. 'My sisters used to come to the snooker club and pull me out to have my tea. I would gulp my tea down and play again.'

At that time, there was no snooker circuit and at 14, Higgins left home to join the Eddie Reavey Racing Stable in Oxfordshire with ambitions to be a jockey.

Jocelyn Reavey remembered Higgins and said: 'He was never doing what he should be doing at the right time and in the right place.

'He seemed to find it hard to focus his energies on to the things we thought he should be doing.

'They [apprentice jockeys] can't ride to start with, so they are supposed to work, cleaning the yard up. Every time you came back in, there was never a sign of a broom or a rake. He was normally at the bookmakers.'

The life of a jockey, Higgins discovered, wasn't for him.

He went to London to work in a paper mill and while there, he rediscovered his appetite for snooker.

'If I had any money, I would go to the hotbeds of snooker,' he said, 'and I used to lose my money, but I was serving an apprenticeship.'

Playing better quality opposition there improved his game and in 1968, Higgins comfortably won the Northern Ireland Amateur Championship.

'Snooker didn't appear to offer a way out,' he said. 'If anyone had suggested I could make a career out of it, I'd have said they were mad.' As it turned out, Higgins was in the right place at the right time ...

'ALEX CAME over from Belfast and was looking for players to play against,' remembered Reg Warland and he reckoned he knew 'a gambler and part-time window cleaner' who could beat him.

Warland, who booked players for exhibitions across the Midlands, knew Higgins had been 'outstanding at amateur level', but fancied he wasn't good enough to beat Brian Cakebread.

The problem was, Cakebread didn't have any money. Between them, Warland and friend Dick Williamson scraped together £40 for him to wager and the match against Higgins went ahead at Morley Working Men's Club in Cakebread's home city of Leeds in 1970.

'We were reasonably confident,' said Warland. 'Brian could make centuries for fun. We were going to stay at Brian's mum's house, but couldn't tell her he was playing snooker for money.

'We had to tell her he had taken a couple of days off from his job at a factory in Leicester and was just back for a visit.'

Higgins took the £40 by winning 4-0, 4-0, 4-1. He gave Cakebread 14 points and then 28 points in the last match. 'Brian said nobody in the world could give him a 28-point start,' said Warland – but Higgins could.

Warland could barely believe what he was watching.

'We had never seen anything like it,' he said. 'It was ferocious, 100-miles-per-hour stuff and we couldn't believe what Alex could do with the cue ball. Back then, the cloths were much heavier and thicker and that made the tables slower. The balls were heavier and the pockets tighter, but he could pot balls and screw the cue ball the length of the table. We had never seen anyone put so much screw and side on the cue ball.'

Warland remembered one screw shot that went wrong, the cue ball jumping off the table and dropping into the glass of a spectator.

Higgins said, 'Sorry babes,' and picked the ball out of the glass.

'He left us penniless,' sighed Warland.

Warland played Higgins himself and said: 'He could be charming and obnoxious in the space of a few hours. In the early days, he was more fun, but was always temperamental.

'He got upset when we were £3 short in a restaurant. He had a tantrum, started punching the bonnet of his girlfriend's car. He would change when he had a drink. He would just flip.'

Warland went to a nightclub with Higgins once – and got thrown out. 'He ended up dancing with a couple of girls,' he said, 'and I think he asked them for a threesome because one of them slapped him, there was a big row and we were all thrown out.'

Reardon remembered an exhibition against Higgins 'in a small theatre in Sheffield and he turned up with two black eyes, had been up all night. I looked at him and thought, "He won't be able to see much out of those two," and he goes and pots everything in sight. Amazing.'

Sometimes, Higgins potted balls by mistake.

'He has more flukes in one match than I get in a year,' wrote Reardon, 'but that's because his style of play allows them to happen. Most players just wobble the ball in the jaws of the pocket when they miss a shot, but Alex misses by a foot and invariably doubles it into the opposite pocket. He's entitled to that, though, because he takes more chances.

'Mind you, he sometimes plays off the table more times than he plays on it. On one occasion he finished up in a street in Preston. He hammered a pink right off the table and down the steps into the corridor. It was hilarious. How he's never broken a ball in half I'll never know, but one thing's for certain: when Alex has finished a session the balls aren't round any more.'

IF HE were to become the youngest world snooker champion, Higgins would have to win six matches over the course of 12 months.

Higgins had to qualify for the 1972 World Championship and left Jackie Rea shaking his head after beating him.

'He does everything wrong – and yet he knocks such a lot in,' shrugged Rea.

Higgins kept knocking them in and faced Rex Williams in a semi-final that went all the way to a deciding 61st frame.

Higgins snatched it after Williams missed a straightforward blue into the middle pocket. 'That blue could have changed the direction of both our careers,' said Williams later.

Higgins faced defending champion John Spencer in the final over the best of 73 frames at Selly Park British Legion.

Phil Yates, subsequently to become a leading journalist and commentator, was there as a nine-year-old.

'All I can remember is smoke hanging over the table,' he said. 'The seating was very rudimentary. We were seated on pallets to give it a tiered effect, there was no television, it was totally different.'

The players had to deal with the disruption of spectators walking past them on their way to the bar and to add to the chaos, the final was played out during a miners' strike and there was a power cut before the evening session on the first day that led to a mobile generator being used to provide light. There was another power cut before play on the fifth evening, leaving Spencer and his wife stuck in a lift!

On the table, the snooker was electrifying.

'I remember how quick Higgins was in relation to Spencer,' said Yates, 'and Spencer was no slouch himself.'

The scores were locked at 21-21 and Higgins won the next six. Spencer got back to within two frames of Higgins at 33-31 before Higgins pulled away.

He won the next two and after Spencer missed in the 68th frame, Higgins mopped up with 94, his highest break of the match, and wrapped up victory with a run of 40.

'Snooker would never be the same again,' wrote Clive Everton years later.

Patsy Fagan, who Higgins replaced as Ireland's leading player, went along with that.

'The turning point was when Higgins came along,' he said. 'He showed that if you take your chances you can win a frame with one visit to the table, you could put a frame to bed straight away. It wasn't like that until 1972.

'The game had been a lot more tactical and people thought snooker was played by old boys who just strolled around the table playing safety shots. They watched Higgins and knew he was different.

'He wasn't looking to make breaks of 20 or 30, he wanted to make centuries. He played magic shots and ran around the table. He made snooker a completely different game.

'Young players like Jimmy White watched him play and thought: "I love the way this fella plays." He wanted to play like Alex Higgins. That's the way it works. Young players learn from great old players. They want to find out how the great players play their shots and work at it until they know how to do it.'

There was little press coverage of Higgins becoming the youngest world snooker champion, at the age of 22 years, 345 days.

(Joe Davis had been the previous youngest, lifting the trophy in 1927 when aged 26 years, 27 days.)

The Times only found room for a 90-word report of Higgins's win over Spencer and elsewhere, it was largely ignored.

Higgins – and snooker – received a welcome boost when ITV screened a documentary, *Hurricane Higgins*, in September 1972.

It followed *Coronation Street* and was the 25th-most-viewed programme of the week.

The excited narrator told viewers Higgins could 'break a frame and pocket every ball inside four minutes, a feat that took the immortal Joe Davis twice as long'.

Higgins said: 'God gave me a gift and I have dedicated myself to that gift. When you're playing well, you can do anything. I can play a shot five or six different ways. It depends how I feel.'

He was full of belief. 'I want to be remembered,' he said. 'I'm the greatest at present.'

The Times drew comparisons with 'Fast' Eddie Felson, the hero of the 1961 Academy Award-winning film *The Hustler*, played by Paul Newman.

ENCOURAGED BY the response to *Hurricane Higgins*, the World Professional Billiards and Snooker Association (WPBSA) decided to make the 1973 World Championship more attractive to audiences and condensed it into a fortnight at Manchester's City Exhibition Halls.

Higgins ran into trouble before he had even struck a ball.

'He had a green suit on, a couple of girls on his arm,' is how John Virgo remembered it. 'Real rock and roll.

'Because he wore a green suit, they fined him £2,000.'

There were extraordinary headlines made during Higgins's quarter-final against Fred Davis.

For John Williams, it was 'the first proper professional match I refereed. I had to borrow a suit and had no britches, so was struggling to keep my trousers up.'

Williams remembered the Exhibition Halls as being 'an old building with a glass roof' and to stop sunlight beaming on to the tables, tarpaulin was draped across the roof. But it cracked the glass ...

'Manchester being Manchester, it rained,' laughed Williams. 'Fred was playing a shot, then turned to me and said: "It's raining." He had felt a drop of water on his hand. We called some workmen, the players went off to the fish and chip shop and 40 minutes later, we were ready to play again.

'The back pages are usually full of football stories, but the next day it was all about how rain stopped play at the snooker.'

Davis was impressed by Higgins.

He said the Irishman was 'a gambler at heart' who 'just ignored the percentages which were stacked against him and knocked them in.

'Besides potting very well, Alex played some extraordinary positional shots. He had the cue power to screw back enormous distances and attacked the game with such an energy and flair that no one quite knew what was coming next.'

Snooker was a different game, according to Davis.

He wrote: 'In the decade or so that [Walter] Donaldson and I were dominating the championship, the pockets tended to be very strict, but they now tended to be, if not actually big, then cut in such a way as to help balls into pockets rather than keeping them out. This inclined to favour potting at the expense of positional play and, on balance, aided the new generation of professionals rather than the old. The change from the Crystalate ball to the lighter and less predictable Super Crystalate, which was used for championship play for the first time in 1973, also had this effect.'

There were more problems after the BBC cameras arrived to cover the semi-finals and final.

The television lights were so bright that Ray Reardon struggled to see in the final against Eddie Charlton, who thrashed Higgins in the last four, and on his insistence, the lights over the audience were switched off. Reardon composed himself to beat Charlton 38-32.

After the World Championship, Higgins headed to Australia to play exhibitions – and cause trouble.

Norman Squire, a popular local professional, was branded 'an old no-hoper' and Higgins was forced to write an apology on toilet paper.

After wrecking his hotel room, Higgins headed to India – where he stayed just one day.

Members of the Bombay Gymkhana Club were offended by Higgins drinking and removing his shirt and he was soon escorted to the airport and told to take the next plane home.

Higgins then came to blows with Graham Miles after losing a match in Wales.

Higgins remembered in his autobiography saying to Miles as he collected his winner's cheque: 'Graham, you're a jammy bald bugger.'

'He took a swing at me and sent me tumbling into the crowd. He missed, but I'd overbalanced. I got my revenge in the dressing room. They had to send a couple of bouncers to pull us apart.'

Miles said: 'It was a clash of personalities. It got under my skin, the way he was performing.'

They clashed again, Miles saying it was 'just a tiff blown up by the press. There was nothing to it really.'

Higgins held himself together rather better at the 1976 World Championship, coming through deciding frames against Cliff Thorburn and John Spencer before grinding out a 20-18 win over Eddie Charlton in the semi-finals.

That set up a final against Reardon, who was aiming for a fourth successive World Championship.

Reardon had played the previous rounds in Middlesbrough, while Higgins had been playing in front of sell-out crowds in Manchester.

The final was staged in Manchester and to avoid Higgins having any unfair advantage, the slate and cloth on the table was changed.

Reardon wasn't happy with either the table or the lighting. The latter was fixed and with Higgins leading 10-9, Reardon insisted the table wasn't adequate.

Higgins later wrote: 'I had every right to say, "Look, you may be world champion, but I'm playing you for your title now. This is the table we've elected to play on and I don't want this table touched." But like a fool I let him have his own way.'

Reardon seemed to be able to manipulate Higgins.

He knew that when Higgins saw a half-chance, the likelihood was, the adrenaline would surge through him and he would take a deep breath and throw his cue at it.

He left Higgins what he called 'tempters. I left it, so if he missed he would be in trouble.'

The most costly miss by Higgins came in the 29th frame and wasn't the result of Reardon leaving a 'tempter'. Rather, Higgins made a baffling choice.

He needed a straightforward red to leave Reardon needing snookers and surely leave himself just a frame behind at 15-14, but for some reason, Higgins chose to play the shot left-handed – and missed.

Higgins seemed resigned to defeat.

Before the final day, he was up all night taking advantage of a complimentary bar in his hotel. Geoff Lomas, Higgins's manager at the time reckoned Alex was drinking until seven o'clock in the morning.

'He was pissed,' remembered Reardon. 'Absolutely. He couldn't see the balls. He was missing easy shots. He was gone.'

The final miss was a pink off its spot in the 43rd frame.

The frame was still winnable for Higgins, but he turned away from the table, offered his hand to Reardon as a sign of his surrender, sat down and lit a cigarette.

Reardon appeared almost embarrassed by the ending. 'I wasn't very happy,' he said years later. 'I wanted to win it fair and square, not because he had drank too much ale.'

Reardon said later: 'I was accused of histrionics, but I won the £6,000 first prize.'

ONE NIGHT, Carol Watterson went to the theatre – and changed snooker history.

'She went to this play with a friend,' remembered husband Mike Watterson, a promoter whose inventions had included the UK Snooker Championships, 'and said: "I have seen a cracking venue for snooker." I said I would have a look. I walked into the auditorium and thought: "Wow! Perfect."'

The venue was the Crucible Theatre in Sheffield and after receiving guarantees from the WPBSA and remortgaging his house, Watterson booked the venue for two weeks for the 1977 World Championship.

'There was nothing like playing there,' remembered Cliff Thorburn. 'I went there to sit in the crowd. I didn't like to sit there. It was too claustrophobic. It was very dramatic.'

Donald Trelford, author of *Snookered* and former editor of *The Observer*, wrote in the programme for the 1986 World Championship, 'The sound of the Crucible is a hiss that clicks.

'The steeply banked seating makes for mesmeric concentration on the altar-like table, tended by black-tied gladiators with finely honed weapons and a red-coated referee in white gloves, all going about their curious, priest-like tasks before a hushed congregation. This aptly named theatre, set in the City of Steel, puts men's characters to the test. The champion is the man who can stay incandescent longest without losing shape.'

Record crowds of more than 20,000 watched the first World Championship at the Crucible and they saw a couple of very dramatic matches. Doug Mountjoy sank a decisive black down the cushion to beat Alex Higgins 13-12 in the first round and in the last eight, Thorburn scraped past Eddie Charlton by winning a 62-minute final frame.

The 53-year-old John Pulman reached the semi-finals where he was beaten by John Spencer 18-16.

Spencer beat Thorburn 25-21 in the final to win the World Championship for a third time, six years after his previous victory.

Snooker was growing – and that hadn't gone unnoticed in Plumstead, where Steve Davis started to think of a possible career change ...

'I HATE STEVE DAVIS'

'PERSONALLY, I hate Steve Davis,' said Alex Higgins, 'but apart from that, he's a very good professional snooker player.'

The tabloid press knew the story here wasn't Higgins calling Davis 'a very good snooker player'.

Reporters needed a response from Davis and he told them, 'Of course I hate Higgins, but I love playing him.'

Davis delivered his words with a smile, playing down the rivalry.

The irony is that though Higgins was the 'People's Champion' and millions wished Davis would lose whoever he was playing, Davis was surely more agreeable company – and fun.

He showed his quick wit when interviewed alongside Higgins.

'Davis sends spectators to sleep,' said Higgins. 'Spectators have no point of contact. How can you relate to a robot? I'd rather have a drink with Idi Amin.'

Davis replied: 'That was because Idi Amin would buy him more drinks.'

Davis said it would be 'strange' for two competitors at the top of a sport to be good friends and even joked Higgins once saved his life.

'I came out of the stage door of a tournament and three blokes set upon me, started beating me up,' said Davis.

'Fortunately for me, Alex came round the corner and said: "That should be enough, lads."'

Davis and Higgins were the Bjorn Borg and John McEnroe of the drinking classes.

Borg was an icy-cool, ruthless tennis champion from Sweden, McEnroe a hot-headed talent who blamed others when he lost. McEnroe was famous for screeching 'You cannot be serious' in his New York accent at umpires when decisions went against him.

Davis was polished, unflappable and emotionless, while Higgins lived in a world of ripped-up betting slips and resentment towards authority.

Clive Everton made the comparison with tennis great Borg after Davis won his first world title in 1981.

He wrote in *The Guardian*: 'In his dedication, temperate habits, appetite for his chosen game, temperament and, in match play, his ability to reduce avoidable mistakes to a minimum, he resembles Bjorn Borg.'

Geoff Lomas, Higgins's manager, said around the same time: 'He [Higgins] astounds me. Higgins represents everything an image shouldn't be, yet it works. This is just an enigma. You can't work it out. It's like McEnroe. He's terribly popular, however badly he behaves.'

Higgins called Davis 'calculating' and it sounded like an insult. The implication was, Davis somehow shouldn't be trusted.

Davis admitted years later that Higgins 'played from the heart' and that wasn't his way. He said: 'He probably felt I didn't play the game with enough panache.'

Higgins needed the gallery as much as he needed to win. Early managers remembered having to drag Higgins away from exhibitions because, as long as there was a crowd, he wanted to entertain them.

Higgins made every manager he ever had tear their hair out, while Davis was just what Barry Hearn was looking for.

BARRY HEARN was born on 19 June 1948 and grew up in Dagenham.

'I always wanted to be rich,' he said.

'My dad was a bus driver who died very young and my mum was a house cleaner.

'The big houses were at the top of the hill. I thought: "They've got more money than me and they must have stuff that needs doing."

'From 12 or 13, I started window cleaning rounds, car cleaning rounds, babysitting rounds. I employed kids from the school and took a turn out of them, so I always had cash – and that gave me that independence.'

Hearn had to accept he wasn't going to become rich by playing sport.

'I grew up wanting to be heavyweight champion of the world,' he said.

'Boxing was the sport that took you out of rags and into riches. I found out I wasn't very good at fighting. It was not a good career move.

'You can't name a sport I haven't done and I was gold medal standard in enthusiasm, but not even bronze medal in ability.

'I gave them all 110 per cent, but God decided sport wasn't for me.'

As a pupil at Buckhurst Hill Grammar School, Hearn entered the Essex Schools Athletics Championship.

He fancied he would have a chance of winning the two-mile walk and though quick enough to be comfortably second, Hearn found himself way behind the leader.

He remembered: 'I was so far behind that there was no way I could catch the guy in front, so I pushed myself to go faster and faster. What happened? I was disqualified almost on the line for "lifting" [breaking into a run], so I didn't even get second.

'At school assembly on the Monday morning, the headmaster said how terrible it was that someone from the school should have been disqualified.

'I could have been second easily, but this was his attitude.'

Later in life, Hearn discovered running.

'I decided to keep fit and someone said, "You should run,"' he said.

'I ran marathons and triathlons around the world. I never won anything, but I was always focused. I could run three hours at a time just looking at a wall. I thought to myself, "I'm not stopping."

'I got down to three hours, 20 minutes [for a marathon] which wasn't bad, but it says more about the character of the person that they persevered.'

Hearn's mother told him once that he should be an accountant. The best houses she cleaned, Barry was told, always belonged to accountants.

'My uncle had a business and he asked his accountant to give me a job,' remembered Hearn. 'From 18 to 21, I didn't go out, but I learned every word of every [accountancy] book. I wasn't going to fail. If you want something enough, you do it.'

The hard work paid off. Hearn went on to be audit manager at KPMG and 'then I got head-hunted to help an investment company to expand and diversify.

'I took them into property, lost a fortune. I took them into garment manufacture, lost a fortune.

'Then I found a chain of snooker halls.

'Bingo!

'The moment I bought them the BBC put snooker on TV and this business was a huge overnight success.

'Everyone said, "You're a genius, how did you see it coming?"

'It was a fluke.'

Hearn developed a fondness for snooker.

'I had no background in the game,' said Hearn, 'but I've always considered myself to be working class and snooker is a working-class game.

'The snooker club was always a dingy place where working-class people convened to swap stories about what's wrong with their lives and life in general.

'I fell in love with the game. It's a great touch-and-feel game, provides more drama than most other sports and every single frame is different.'

JEAN DAVIS wanted her eldest son to work in a bank, but her husband had other ideas.

'It was my father's love of snooker that led me down that path,' said Steve Davis.

'He didn't push me, but it was his hobby, so I followed in his footsteps.

'I was getting a positive affirmation that playing snooker wasn't a bad thing to do. At one time, it might have been a bad idea, but nobody at home was telling me to stop playing snooker and go out and get a job.'

Davis played at the Lucania club in Romford, owned by Hearn.

'I met Steve when he was 18 years old,' said Hearn.

'He didn't have any personality, but he had a steely-eyed determination that had been instilled by his father, Bill.

'He was Steve's coach and mentor. Bill wasn't a great player, but he was a great coach and instilled a practice regime.

'He read a book by Joe Davis about how to play snooker and he followed that word for word.

'He travelled with him for 40 years. Bill was always there chomping on a cigar, drinking a pint of lager and making sure Steve kept his head still. That was the most important thing.'

Davis joked he didn't have any distractions from snooker.

'If you're born ugly, ginger hair, bit of dandruff, no personality, it was very unlikely as a teenager you would want to go out to nightclubs,' he said.

'You would much prefer to be in a dark room without mirrors practising knocking a white ball up and down the spots for eight hours a day. That was how you got good at something.'

Davis got very good at snooker.

'Steve was a total machine,' said Hearn, 'and he was a secret.

'He was unheard of and unbeatable – what a combination! We would travel the country playing anyone and no one had heard of him back then. No one could beat him, either.

'I would pay him £25 and a cut of the winnings.

'We called him "The Nugget" because you could bet your last tenner on him and still be sure you were going to get paid. You could have bet £1 million on him and he wouldn't care. He just loved playing the game.'

Hearn wanted to test the talented teenager to the full.

He said: 'We would bring the top players down and we would play them for money. This was work experience you couldn't buy.

'We had 300 people sitting in a room with no windows, no fire exit and in those days, pretty well everyone smoked. We would gamble among ourselves. The only person who didn't bet was Steve Davis.'

Davis played Higgins in Romford around 1976 when he was a 19-year-old amateur and Higgins was among the world's elite.

'I've never seen so much excitement in a room,' remembered Davis. 'Alex was getting stick from the crowd.

'He would stand up and chalk his cue, as if he's going to play the next shot and that puts a lot of pressure on you. He's saying "You're going to miss this one."'

Davis didn't miss many that night. He won the match and Hearn remembered: 'We made loads of money and he [Higgins] stormed out.'

Higgins made a comment to Bill Davis, Steve's father, that stayed with the winner.

Higgins told him: 'It's OK for your son, he's got Barry behind him. I've got nobody.'

Davis said years later: 'Someone like that needs someone to protect them, not only from the outside world, but from themselves.'

Davis turned professional in October 1978 and five months later, he met Higgins in a best-of-65-frames challenge match, held over four days at the Lucania club in Romford.

Davis remembered: 'Higgins was so confident he would beat me that he went off and put a lot of money on himself ... what he didn't take into account was that I know the table and that he was stepping into a minefield.

'He conceded at the end of the sixth session when the score was 31-18. He simply turned to the crowd and told them not to come back the next day because he wouldn't be there.

'Then he charged down to Barry's office on the ground floor and shouted at everyone in sight. When he stormed out, we thought that was the last we'd see of him.

'When we turned up the next morning, who should be there but Alex, apologising profusely for everything that had happened the day before and raring to do his best on the table.'

Higgins's best wasn't enough. Davis won 33-23 and recalled later that every one of the 56 frames played featured a break of 40 or more. The top break was a 132 by Higgins.

'ALEX WAS everything Davis wasn't,' said Hearn and the snooker-watching public got to choose who they preferred at the 1980 World Championship.

There, Davis met Higgins in the quarter-finals.

In the build-up to the best-of-25-frames match, it was Davis, rather than Higgins, who was attracting the media's attention.

Davis, who had made a first-round exit on his Crucible debut 12 months earlier, beat defending champion Terry Griffiths in the second round and 'The next day I had a film crew following me to the dry cleaners.'

Davis had another surprise when he discovered Higgins wasn't the carefree 'Hurricane' of legend. He thought more and was able to draw mistakes from Davis.

'He would snooker me, I would get out of it and he would put me in another and clear up,' remembered Davis.

Higgins ran out a 13-9 winner, but went on to lose the final to Cliff Thorburn.

From 7-3 up, Higgins lost 18-16, saying afterwards he lost focus when he was ahead and sought to entertain the crowd rather than knuckle down and win the match. Thorburn wasn't entirely happy with this interpretation. 'I beat him,' said Thorburn. Higgins hadn't beaten himself.

Higgins and Davis met each other again six months later, in the final of the UK Championship at Preston Guild Hall.

BBC Television presenter David Vine told viewers 'their approach to the game is very different' and from the opening shots, Higgins appeared to be in a self-destructive mood.

He started the match with a careless break that gave Davis a shot at a red he would have expected to sink. He missed and Higgins obligingly offered him an even simpler pot with his next shot. The nudge into the middle pocket would have been converted by an average club player and Davis turned the gift into a 69 break that sealed the opening frame.

Davis pulled away to a 16-6 victory, securing his first major title.

Higgins was gracious in defeat – to a point. 'Steve did play well,' he said in front of a packed crowd, 'and when you play well, you do get the run of the balls.'

That brought a few cries of derision from Davis's supporters in the crowd, but the champion put a finger to his lips to silence them.

THE PRIZE Davis and Hearn wanted most was the World Championship.

'We would talk about winning the world title and changing the sport,' remembered Hearn.

Higgins was in mischievous mood when interviewed by the BBC during Davis's first-round match against 18-year-old debutant Jimmy White at the 1981 World Championship.

He wasn't impressed by what he had seen of 7/2 tournament favourite Davis or anyone else, saying there's 'not much to beat', before writing off his own chances because he was moving house and then predicting the champion would be either himself, Davis or White.

Davis held off White to win 10-8 and faced Higgins in the second round. The key frame was the 17th. Higgins opened it with 47 to give himself a chance to trim the gap to a single frame at 9-8, but Davis responded with a 45 for 10-7 and went on to win 13-8.

Davis met the defending champion in the semi-finals.

Only weeks before the start of his World Championship defence, Cliff Thorburn had been paid handsomely by Hearn to play Davis in an exhibition match.

Davis thumped him 6-0, a scoreline Hearn hoped would stay with the Canadian at the Crucible.

The World Championship clash would be harder for Davis.

Higgins had nicknamed Thorburn 'The Grinder' during the previous year's World Championship and Davis discovered why. Davis, a winner of four major titles during the 1980/81 season, went an hour without potting a ball as Thorburn turned a 6-4 deficit into an 8-6 lead.

The match restarted with a Union Jack flag draped over the balcony by a group who identified themselves as the 'Romford Mafia' and the crowd were cheered by Davis reducing the gap to 10-9.

Thorburn was on course for the 20th frame – and an 11-9 lead in the best-of-31-frames match – with three colours remaining.

Three times, Thorburn was distracted at crucial moments. Firstly, someone in the crowd whistled, then a plastic cup crackled and a match was struck.

'Not our doing,' insisted Hearn of moments that helped turn the match his player's way.

Davis won the frame to level at 10-10 and thrust his fist triumphantly towards his supporters who, Terry Smith later wrote, 'voiced their approval with a roar never before heard at a snooker tournament'.

Better was to follow for the Romford Mafia as Davis went 11-10 ahead.

In the 22nd frame, Thorburn was left needing eight snookers on the pink and black, and thinking the frame was won, Davis raised a fist to his supporters and went over to shake Thorburn's hand.

Thorburn refused.

He remembered: 'I indicated I was going to play on and went to address the cue ball.

'I imitated Steve's habit of stepping away from the table to take a sip of water, addressed the cue ball and then, without striking it, walked across to him to offer my handshake.

'When we got backstage, I said: "You're an arrogant bastard, Davis. I'll be looking for you tomorrow."

'When I'd cooled down I felt bad about what I had done and I apologised on television the next day.'

Nevertheless, Thorburn was rattled. He didn't win another frame, the match ending after 14½ hours when Davis knocked in a pink that was hanging over a corner pocket.

The final was against Doug Mountjoy, a former Welsh miner who had turned professional at 34 years old after winning the 1976 World Amateur Championship in Johannesburg, South Africa.

Months later, Mountjoy won the first major professional tournament he entered, edging out Ray Reardon on the last two colours in the 13th and deciding frame of the Benson & Hedges Masters Final.

Reardon stood in Mountjoy's way again in the semi-finals of the 1981 World Championship and Mountjoy went through 16-10, aided by a championship-high break of 145 in the 12th frame.

That set up a best-of-35-frames final against Davis that Hearn said 'wasn't a game of snooker. It was me and Steve against the world. We would be unbeatable – provided he won this match.'

Davis did win it, 18-12, in front of a television audience that peaked at 15.6 million, and was left bruised by Hearn's celebratory hug.

Hearn said 40 years on: 'I still think about it every day. We beat the world. I have never felt what I felt in 1981.'

Mountjoy shrugged: 'It probably would have made me a millionaire if I had won. It made Steve Davis a millionaire instead.'

Days later, television cameras visited the 23-year-old from Plumstead who was described as 'the biggest earner in British sport' and found him happily living at home with his parents and playing computer games with his teenage brother, Keith.

'The world was going crazy around me when I walked down the high street,' said nerd-do-well Davis. 'I went from being unknown to being well known and it was a real shock to the mind.

'You can't prepare somebody for that and it's down to the individual how you cope. It was totally surreal, a strange world you can never quite get your head around. You can give someone training in areas such as the media, but you can't give them training for what happens.

'It helps if you have a sense of humour and don't think too much of yourself. It's hard when plenty of people are telling you how fantastic you are. But people at my local snooker club would soon shoot me down in flames. Nobody is bigger than anyone else there. Everyone just takes the piss and has a laugh.'

To the gamblers, chancers and wide boys at his local club, Davis was known as, among other things, 'Personality Minus'.

Spitting Image, the satirical Sunday-night puppet show, called him Steve 'Interesting' Davis and showed him trying to perfect drinking water in between frames. 'Up to the lips, sip and down,' he repeated.

The press speculated Davis's perfectionism would earn £600,000 in 1981, a year in which he repeatedly beat Higgins.

There was a semi-final in the Jameson International Open in Derby that Davis won in a deciding 17th frame and later that year, he had the satisfaction of beating Higgins in front of his home crowd at the Ulster Hall, in the Northern Ireland Classic. That result led the *Belfast Telegraph* to write Higgins 'must surely be wondering when he will beat the tall Londoner in top-class competition'.

THERE SEEMED very little chance of Higgins winning the 1982 World Championship, a decade after he had lifted the trophy.

The following month Sunday tabloid the *News of the World* reported he had been issued with death threats.

Hearn said at the time: 'I've been waiting for Higgins to be destroyed for years. He's looking worse and worse.

There's nothing on him. Sores all over his face. But the fact is: People like watching the process. This is what I think is one of the biggest things in our game.'

Higgins made an early exit in Warrington and afterwards told the press he would 'blow the game apart to the highest bidder'. That was followed by stories of a £1,000-a-week drug habit and a suicide bid.

He was struggling to even win an exhibition match and so poor was his form, manager Geoff Lomas tried to rebuild his confidence by paying friends to lose to him. Higgins, he reckoned, 'couldn't pot a ball'.

Higgins opened his heart to a television interviewer, saying he was suffering with 'nervous exhaustion. The pressure, the travelling, I'm sick of it. My game's suffering.'

Harvey Lisberg was brought in in a management role to help Higgins and remembered that he 'put him in a hospital to dry him out. People used to bring him vodka, he tried to get off with the nurses. The chief doctor said, "What a horrid little man."

'The good news was, Alex came out 80 per cent improved. He had a chance.'

The chances of Higgins increased after Tony Knowles dumped out defending champion Davis 10-1 in what is still remembered as one the great shocks in World Championship history.

'Everyone was telling me I was the best player,' said Davis, 'and then it collapsed.'

It collapsed for No. 2 seed Cliff Thorburn as well, the 1980 champion crashing out in the first round to Jimmy White, 10-4.

Higgins held it together to beat Jim Meadowcroft in the first round and nudge past Mountjoy 13-12 to set up a quarter-final against Willie Thorne.

Higgins and Thorne both made front-page headlines ahead of that match.

Higgins found himself there after relieving himself in a plant pot following a late-night practice session and when a backstage lighting man objected to his idea of watering the plants, there was a scuffle.

The red-tops also revealed Thorne had been having an affair with a married woman.

For a couple of decades, Thorne was one of snooker's most recognisable characters. He had the drooping moustache, clubbed-seal eyes and ho-hum geniality of a favourite uncle.

Often during matches, Thorne would look for family and friends in the audience when he found the run of the balls perplexing and such was his popularity, he always found a comforting face there.

Reg Warland was there from the start. As a 12-year-old, he played with Willie upstairs in the Shoulder of Mutton pub on the rough-and-ready Braunstone estate in Leicester that Willie's parents ran.

'Willie should have had the best temperament of all the players after what he went through,' reckoned Reg. 'But he had to cope with life as well as snooker. He was always betting and owing money and it must have been very hard to focus on snooker.'

What Thorne went through at the age of 15 was his snooker initiation at Osborne's Snooker Club in Leicester city centre, a short walk from the bustling marketplace.

Market traders – including Barry Lineker, father of Gary – would leave their stalls and be drawn to the thrill and danger of Osborne's. Every now and then, the police would call in asking for a well-known character that nobody had ever seen. Obviously.

'It was a real education,' said Warland. 'There were villains, market traders, hard men, con men ... There was a smell, a feel to the place. It was so exciting.'

'I used to lose my 2s 6d pocket money in there,' remembered Thorne. 'Looking back, that's probably where the gambling started, losing a few pence on a game.'

Gambling would cost Thorne thousands of pounds over the years.

Friends who went to York races with him said he lost £250,000 in a week and he confessed in one of his autobiographies that he once lost £150,000 on a football match.

THERE WERE other ways to be separated from your money at Osborne's ...

'I remember someone saying, "If anyone wants a tie, pop to the Gents,"' said Warland. 'He had a tie rack there that had obviously just been pinched from Marks & Spencer.'

Competition on the snooker table was tough and Warland remembers a character known as 'Countesthorpe Ken'.

'Every match he played was decided by the last three colours,' said Reg, 'and Ken would always win. He would beat them, then as he was collecting his winnings he would be charming and say: "I thought you had me there. Shall we play again?"'

Warland added: 'Willie built his reputation in Osborne's. You had to be good. There were a lot of good players playing for big money. Willie lost a lot of matches, but stuck at it. He learned how to hold his own.'

But the one player he couldn't beat was London-based Irishman Patsy Fagan.

Warland remembers 100 people crowding round the table when Thorne and Fagan pitted wits, winning and losing hundreds of pounds. 'Everyone in the place was betting on those matches,' he said.

John Virgo and Paul Medati were other renowned money players who visited Osborne's and when Thorne wasn't playing them, Brian Cakebread was helping him develop the fluent break-building that took him to the English snooker and billiards titles at under-16 level.

Aged 21, Thorne became the youngest-ever professional.

Osborne's changed when it moved to another part of the city – 'The place lost its edge,' said Warland – and along with his brother and mother, Thorne went on to set up his own snooker club in the centre of Leicester where Gary Lineker was a regular.

He would head there after a morning's training with Leicester City Football Club.

Lineker could play and reached the final of the Leicestershire Doubles, partnering Danny Gunn.

In the final, they faced Reg Warland and Geoff Worrall.

'Gary was a 100-break player,' said Warland. 'We knew we had to keep him quiet.'

Gunn did most of the potting and Lineker got his hands on the trophy.

Lineker once estimated he was on the receiving end of 38 maximums made by Thorne in practice, but when the television cameras were on him, the demons in Thorne's mind demanded more attention.

He admitted once: 'I was like a racehorse that's good over the gallops, but not as good on the course.

'The will to win was always there, but I wasn't as confident under pressure as I was when the pressure was off. You twitch a bit more when the pressure is on and that's difficult to cope with in a game like snooker.'

Thorne handled the pressure well enough in that quarter-final against Higgins to compile a championship-high break of 143, but was chasing the Irishman from early in the match and was eventually beaten 13-10.

That sent Higgins through to a best-of-31-frames semi-final against White, whose victory over Kirk Stevens in the last eight had made him the youngest player to ever reach that stage in the World Championship.

At 15-13 ahead, White was only one frame away from the final. Higgins pegged back the 29th frame with a break of 72 and needed to produce something similar when he came to the table trailing 59-0 in the next.

There were six reds left, so a possible 75 points were available to him, but the pink's path to the corner pockets was blocked, the black was nestling unhelpfully near the baulk colours and on top of that, there was the pressure.

'If you miss, you're dead,' was how Higgins put it later.

He knew any slight misjudgement would cost him the match and as he looked up and down the table. Higgins, moving with all the ease of someone who has an itch they can't reach, smiled to himself and licked his lips at the challenge facing him.

He started with a simple enough red left hanging over the pocket by White's miss, then smacked in a long green and took the cue ball around the angles to nudge a troublesome red away from the cushion and over the middle pocket.

After stabbing another red along the top cushion and into the corner pocket, Higgins took the cue ball curving beyond the baulk line and left it perfectly placed to roll up behind the yellow on its spot and lay a snooker. 'I was in no mood for snookers,' he would tell reporters later and, seizing the moment, Higgins instead rattled in a long black to get it back on its spot.

'He could have snookered me,' said White. 'He rolled the black into the corner pocket ... the gamble paid off. The black was on its spot, making his task that bit easier.'

Another red disappeared and Higgins took aim at a difficult blue that he had to steer into one of the pockets at the baulk end of the table.

'He has to get this,' said commentator Jack Karnehm, 'or the match could be over.'

Higgins flashed a glance at the scoreboard and then sent the blue hurtling into the top right-hand pocket with a flourish of his cue.

'I'm sitting in my seat and a couple of times I'm thinking, "I'm coming back to the table,"' remembered White, 'but he pulled off those shots, one after the other.'

After another long red was buried into the same pocket, all the half-chances had been taken and Higgins had worked his way into position. Pausing only occasionally to look at the scoreboard and grin at John Spencer in the commentary box, he mopped up the remaining two reds and took the colours off their spots to complete a break of 69 that sent the match into a 31st and deciding frame.

His reaction – and that of the crowd – after that break suggested the match was over and following a swift cigarette and break of 59 in the final frame, it was.

'I couldn't just shake his hand,' remembered Higgins. 'I had to hug him as if to say: "Sorry, babe, but you'll have your day."'

Higgins and White formed the sort of bond prize-fighters form after pushing each other to the brink for 12 gruelling rounds.

'He took defeat well and we became soulmates after that,' said Higgins.

White said years later: 'Every time I do an exhibition throughout the world they put that 69 clearance on the screen. It's supposed to be about me doing a show that night.'

The final was a repeat of the 1976 final, Higgins facing Reardon.

Higgins ripped his tie off before the opening frame, Reardon nodded and smiled at the referee and crowd, and gently rubbed his knuckles on the table.

Higgins led 15-12; Reardon got it back to 15-15.

'At 15-15, the guy who left the table was a loser,' said Reardon. 'The guy who came out wasn't the guy who went in.

'He'd taken something. He was tested. The test was mislaid. Don't ask me where it went. We never heard any more about it. What a shame. But the guy who came back wasn't the guy who left the floor.'

The revived Higgins won the next three frames, clinching the World Championship with a 135 clearance in the 33rd frame to spark scenes of celebrations that have stayed in the memory of everyone who saw them.

Higgins, the hell-raising 'Hurricane' and bad boy of snooker, wept tears of joy and sobbed 'My baby' as wife Lynn and 18-month-old daughter Lauren stepped out of the audience to congratulate their hero.

'I'm very happy,' said Higgins. 'I will die a happy man.'

He went home to Ireland with White and Geoff Lomas to celebrate.

White said: 'Every town we went to, we would arrange for the nightclubs to stay open and we would go into every one of them.'

That was followed by a nationwide exhibition tour featuring Higgins playing White. White said: 'The promoter ran off with the money, all the ticket money. We decided to do it for the fans for nothing.'

The driver who was taking Higgins and White around the country found out about the promoter disappearing and fearing he wouldn't be paid, he kidnapped the World Championship trophy as insurance.

White remembered: 'The guy said, "I'm keeping this trophy until I get my money."'

Higgins ended up paying him £250, joking to reporters: 'I'm the only one paying out any money ... it's costing me a fortune being world champion.'

'I STOOD there with him and the cup,' said the world champion's wife, Lynn Higgins, 'and thought: "My problems are going to start."

'He was mixing with more famous people, he was in London and he got into bad habits.

'He'd get up at lunchtime, want to have breakfast when we'd all had lunch and then he'd sit there in front of the television. It was TV, his cigarettes, his newspaper and his beer.'

Daughter Lauren remembered after her father's death, 'Dad would throw whatever he could through windows in drunken rages – the TV, silverware, even [son] Jordan's skateboard once.

'Police became regular visitors. We became quite friendly with them – I remember playing with their badges.'

Higgins headed to the Crucible Theatre in April 1983 as the world champion and No. 1 seed.

There was friction during his second-round match against Willie Thorne.

Thorne said Higgins accused him of cheating. Higgins answered: 'I didn't call him a cheat, but I told him I don't like people who would sell their own grandmother for two bob.'

Thorne said: 'Somebody should do something about it. He gets away with murder all the time.'

Higgins held himself together better than Thorne to win 13-11, but was then accused of flicking a 'V' sign at referee John Williams during his quarter-final with Bill Werbeniuk.

Tony Knowles was quoted in the *News of the World* as saying Higgins needed 'a good thump right between the eyes'.

He added: 'None of the players like him. He's like a spoiled child, always wanting his own way. He's always been a pain in the neck.'

Higgins faced Davis in the semi-finals.

Higgins told reporters during the match that he was living on a bizarre diet of honey, lager and vitamin pills, explaining: 'I need energy. I just don't eat properly.'

It didn't do him much good.

Davis powered into a 9-2 lead and then someone rang the Crucible and said: 'If Davis wins ten frames, he will be shot.'

Police searched spectators and used a metal detector to hunt for a possible weapon, but found nothing and the match restarted after a 35-minute delay.

Davis wasn't told of the threat until after he completed a 16-5 win and faced the press with two minders carrying a toy machine gun each.

Davis said: 'I knew something was up in the interval – everyone was so hushed. I guessed it wasn't just a bomb scare. We'll have to have sandbags around the table.'

Higgins dismissed the caller as 'sick'.

Davis showed no mercy to Thorburn in the final, completing an 18-6 thrashing with a session to spare.

THE SUMMER of 1983 was very different for Davis and Higgins. The world champion helped Margaret Thatcher's Conservative Party celebrate being re-elected to government, while Higgins fought to save his marriage.

He went to Majorca with Lynn in the hope they would be able to patch up their differences, but there was no reconciliation and Higgins ended up taking an overdose that left him in a coma for 48 hours.

He checked himself out of Cheadle Hospital and Lynn said later: 'He said they were all nuts and there was nothing wrong with him.'

Reporters felt Higgins looked unwell when he arrived in Preston for the start of the UK Championship in November 1983 and he appeared to be heading for an early exit when Murdo McLeod won the opening four frames of their first-round match.

Higgins turned the match around to win 9-6 and said during his semi-final victory over Terry Griffiths that he had been reconciled with Lynn.

Even so, Davis started the final a 4/6 favourite having lost just 12 frames in four previous matches. So well was Davis playing, one punter reportedly bet his entire life savings on him beating Higgins and that looked a good investment when Davis went 7-0 ahead in the best-of-31-frames match.

One of Higgins's close friends, Andrew Chandler, a pro golfer on the European Tour, helped him through the crisis. He said: 'I made sure he went back to the hotel, that he had a meal and that we talked about everything under the sun except snooker.

'I can't tell him how to win snooker matches in terms of skill, but I do understand the mental process.'

By the end of the first day, Higgins was back in the match, trailing by a single frame at 8-7, and the second day was Lauren's second birthday, an occasion that was sure to give him further motivation.

Higgins went on to take a shock 14-12 lead – only two frames away from victory – but Davis took the next three.

Higgins gave the match the climax it deserved by forcing a deciding 31st frame.

Twelve months earlier he lost the deciding frame to Terry Griffiths in the final, but this time, Higgins held his nerve rather better.

Davis went for a long red – and missed. Higgins made only five, but left the cue ball safe – and soon forced another error from Davis.

It looked a match-winning opportunity. Higgins asked for the cue ball to be cleaned as he gathered his thoughts and weighed up his options. He only made a break of 21 before running out of position, but when Davis came back to the table, he was snookered behind the green and the reds were spread invitingly at the other end of the table.

Even for a player of Davis's calibre, it would be tough to escape the snooker and leave it safe. He came off two cushions to nudge a red, but left Higgins a choice of pottable balls.

He chose a red into the middle pocket, added a pink and there was the promise of more.

Higgins stopped to think twice, three times occasionally, over his choice of shot – and the break built steadily.

It reached 36 when Higgins stabbed a red into the middle pocket, leaving Davis needing snookers.

The likelihood was, Davis wouldn't get a chance to lay any snookers. Higgins was in a groove. The break broke down at 44, but there was no way back for Davis.

He tried a safety shot that left a red hanging over a corner pocket and Higgins made it disappear to cheers from the crowd. The pink followed before Higgins missed, but the match was won.

Davis offered his hand in resignation and there were tears from Higgins, just a handshake and a pat on the back for the loser.

Higgins had pulled off what David Emery of the *Daily Express* called 'the greatest escape act snooker has seen'.

Higgins said afterwards: 'Everyone knows there's little love lost between Steve and me ... Players were beginning to live in Steve's shadow, but he will have to fear me now.

'My good lady has spurred me on. I know what I can be. It's a matter of discipline.'

Davis said of Higgins years later: 'The occasions when things were going really badly in his life maybe he could enjoy the beauty of having the freedom to just play the game.'

MOST TIMES Davis played Higgins, Davis won.

Four times they met in the first half of the 1984/85 season and Davis won them all.

In total, he had won 13 of their 15 matches on the circuit going into the 1985 Benson & Hedges Masters.

Davis always said that whenever he played Higgins, he also played the crowd and that was clearly the case when they faced each other in the first round at a highly charged Wembley Conference Centre.

'When you played Alex Higgins, the people who used to come along to support Alex weren't necessarily snooker fans,' remembered Davis years later.

'They liked Alex Higgins playing snooker – they were far more vocal than most of the snooker fans were.'

The sell-out crowd clearly identified more with the chain-smoking Higgins than the water-sipping Davis and as the players returned from a break to play the deciding ninth frame, Higgins was cheered and Davis was booed.

That ninth frame went down to the colours and a safety exchange on the blue.

It was Davis who blinked first, leaving Higgins a thin cut into the bottom pocket.

The blue disappeared and the cue ball went around the table and stopped at the right moment to enable Higgins to roll in the match-winning pink.

'We're fucking back!' he roared and, as Neal Foulds remembered it, around '20 to 30' supporters rushed to congratulate him.

'John Lazarus, the tournament director, came out to disperse the crowd,' said Foulds, 'and after they'd gone he found out someone had taken his wallet!'

BARRY HEARN kept adding players to his Matchroom stable and giving them personalities.

'Davis, you wear white shirts, black suits, you won't say anything, you're the boring one,' he told his star performer.

'Willie Thorne, all you talk about is gambling all the time anyway so talk about it on air.

'Thorburn, you're "The Grinder", the cool dude; Griffiths, you're from Wales, you think you can sing, so you hum all the time when you're playing and you comb your hair because you're fastidious about your hair.'

'People can say "I like him" or "I don't like him", I don't care. As long as you watch them.'

He knew people would watch Higgins, but he didn't want him.

'Alex wouldn't work in my environment,' he said. 'Alex could have brought down the whole empire I was trying to build.'

Higgins was unquestionably the biggest crowd-puller in snooker, but while he went to exhibitions by train and bus and was paid hundreds of pounds, Davis drove to exhibitions in a Porsche bought for him by Hearn and charged £1,500.

The fact was, Davis won trophies and had Hearn behind him, while Higgins didn't.

Davis–Higgins remained the biggest match in snooker, one of the biggest matches in British sport. Such was the demand to see them play each other, they went on a ten-date exhibition tour of Scotland together that was always likely to be uncomfortable for Davis.

The problems started on the opening night when Higgins saw a stand in the venue's foyer offering to sell signed posters of himself and Davis.

Davis wrote: 'Alex walked in, saw the stand and scattered our posters all over the floor. He didn't like the fact we were selling Alex Higgins posters and he wasted no time informing the crowd he would only sign those posters bought from him.'

He said Higgins 'continued to be obnoxious throughout the ten days. He gave everyone hell. We stayed in the same hotel, but I made sure I kept well away. The only time you get a good word from Alex is when he's winning and although he played fairly well, I won quite comfortably.'

Davis remembered one exhibition where he watched Higgins go on stage after losing and tell the crowd to cheers that he would be back like 'Muhammad Ali'. Davis found the episode 'hilarious'.

Less amusing for Davis was the time he spent sitting next to Higgins on a plane. He said: 'The only time we were together for any length of time was on an early flight to Canada and I was so nervous on the flight, having to spend seven or eight hours on a plane trapped with Alex – and he probably felt the same.

'I knocked a beer all over me. I was a gibbering wreck and he was so nice. We had a good chat. But a few beers later it was different …'

THE 1986 UK Championship at Preston Guild Hall was a low point for Higgins.

He reached the quarter-finals with a 9-7 victory over Mike Hallett. Higgins had left the arena at 7-7 and returned to play two inspired frames of snooker. Higgins took some of the joy out of his victory by saying snooker had 'lost its magic' and that the pockets were too big, meaning that 'anyone can make a century'.

Worse was to follow after Paul Hatherell, the tournament director, asked Higgins to take a drugs test …

Ann Yates, who was in charge of the press room that night, remembered: 'He'd obviously had a good drink and was spoiling for a fight after being asked to take the test by Hatherell.

'The next thing was that the doctor appeared looking shaken and said he had been threatened physically in the cubicle.'

Higgins returned to the players' room, complaining he had been victimised and had taken a test earlier in the tournament.

'I tried to explain that the tests were predetermined long before the tournament had begun,' said Yates, 'but he would not listen. He bleated that his life was a misery because his wife had left him again, taking their two children with her.'

Higgins demanded a private meeting with David Harrison, the tournament administrator.

'After a few minutes and some heated words, there was an almighty crash as Alex shoved David into a filing cabinet against a partition wall,' remembered Yates.

'He pushed Alex off him angrily, sending him across the room, still clutching his pint.

'Some time had elapsed by now and Hatherell was getting curious, not knowing what had transpired.

'He wandered back into the office to see what was going on and when Higgins saw him, he dropped the glass, grabbed Paul by the tie and smashed him with his head by the side of his eye, opening a nasty cut.

'With the blood pouring out and splattering Paul's shirt, Higgins tightened his grip on the tie and started to choke him.'

Higgins was then faced with a security guard.

Yates said: 'There was a stand-off for a moment as Higgins hesitated, then stormed back to the players' room, where John Virgo, John Spencer and Del Simmons attempted to calm him down.'

Virgo remembered: 'He wasn't for calming down. He was looking to take it out on somebody.'

Higgins punched a hole in the wall and another three in the door before storming into the corridor and picking up a pile of dinner plates the caterers had left behind.

Yates said: 'He started skimming them at us like flying saucers and we had to duck all over the place to avoid being hit.'

After he ran out of plates to throw, Higgins started throwing his fists – until security officer Frank Baker wrapped his arms around him.

'But he was way out of control. There was a huge ball of foam in his mouth and I'd never seen anything like it my life,' said Yates.

'Then Higgins started stubbing his cigarette out on Frank's hand. That was it. Virgo told Harrison to call the police because we had no other option.

'Alex was dragged from the building, face up and heels dragging, by two police officers – one a woman – but not before he gave us a urine sample, which tested negative anyway.'

Higgins was allowed to play his quarter-final against Wayne Jones and he told the press the night before: 'I'm certainly in the right frame of mind [to play the match]. I hope my public comes and supports me.'

Though he was allowed to stay in the tournament, Higgins would surely be handed a sizeable fine and a lengthy ban.

'Can you face life without snooker, Alex?' he was asked.

'Can snooker face life without me?'

The crisis seemed to focus Higgins on his snooker and he won the first six frames of his quarter-final against Jones.

He went through 9-3, but it was unlikely Higgins would reach the final.

Davis was standing in his way and in their previous four matches, Higgins had won a total of just six frames.

The semi-final was the best of 17 frames and Davis won it 9-3.

'I thought it would be more of a match,' said the winner afterwards. 'We haven't had any of our good battles lately.'

Davis went on to beat Neal Foulds 16-7 in the final, while Higgins was fined £12,000 and banned for five tournaments for his assault.

'It will give me six months to enjoy three rounds of golf a week,' Higgins smirked when interviewed by Terry Wogan.

'Of course I'm sorry. I'm sorry it wasn't defused quicker.'

To escape the media spotlight, Higgins headed off to Oliver Reed's mansion for a week before doing a television interview.

'On the morning I was due to leave,' Higgins wrote, 'Ollie dragged me out of bed at the crack of dawn and insisted that we have a farewell drink.

'He poured a half-pint glass of whisky and ordered me to down it in one.

'Now when Ollie orders you to do that, you do it. No questions asked.

'The tricky bastard had put most of a bottle of his new wife's perfume in the glass and I, like a fool, downed most of it before I realised. Too late, I tried to bring it up, but couldn't.

'I was sick hours later and for a few days afterwards and the poor presenter had to interview me that morning while I silently belched.

'I'm told he even remarked to the director through his lapel mic that I smelled like a goddess.'

'YOU CAN'T BUY YOUTH'

JIMMY WHITE'S changing room looked how you might expect Jimmy White's changing room to look.

Next to the packet of 20 Benson & Hedges cigarettes on his dressing table, *The Sun* newspaper lay open at the racing page and at the centre of it all was White himself; genial, chatty, seated for a minute, then back on his feet lighting a cigarette, fidgety and preoccupied.

This was the scene backstage before White took on Ken Doherty in the Premier League at Warwick University in 2010.

Many in the audience that night had watched White grow up; some may have remembered him as a teenager in an early interview when he spelled out his ambitions.

He said: 'I just want to be world champion and enjoy life.'

White enjoyed playing snooker. He said once: 'When I'm out there playing and I see a tasty looking shot, I can't refuse it. Sometimes I try something chancy and it doesn't come off, but when it does that's the biggest buzz of all.'

The public loved the way White played the game. *The Times* outlined White's appeal when they wrote: 'He has everything the people could wish for. A great crashing adventurousness with the balls, staggering skills, awesome power ... He makes snooker seem a gay, chivalrous thing, one in which a young man could happily toss away his life with a smile: if Harry Hotspur had been a snooker player, he would have been Jimmy White of Tooting.'

The public who loved him felt the pain of White's defeats deeply.

'There were often times when I had fans in my room and I'd be consoling them – grown men, giants of men, crying and bawling because I had lost,' White said. 'So that was a bit bizarre.'

White first dived into his local snooker club, Zan's in Tooting, to escape a street skirmish that was getting out of hand. 'The place fascinated me long before the game did,' he wrote in his autobiography.

Zan's was where characters such as Victor Yo, Flash Bob and Johnny the Arab would spend their days hustling and gambling.

White started playing and by the age of 13, he had made his first century break and come to the attention of a local taxi driver known as Dodgy Bob.

He reckoned that White and 15-year-old Tony Meo could earn well playing money matches around London – and he was proved right.

White once borrowed 30 bob from his father and by the end of the day he had turned it into £1,000.

This was an exciting, but dangerous life.

White described the company he kept at the time as 'villains and thieves' and he saw someone shot in the legs at a club in Wimbledon and heard of 'a grass' being stoned to death with snooker balls.

White escaped the back streets to win the English Amateur Championship in 1979.

That form earned him selection for the Home Internationals in Prestatyn, Wales, the following year.

Manager Henry West told White not to drink because it would enrage the head of the amateur body, Bill Cottier.

Cottier, White was told, had the power to 'make or break' his snooker career.

White vowed not to touch a drop, apart from a half of lager that Cottier spotted him drinking. 'Jimmy White, you should be ashamed of yourself,' he said, 'you won't be playing today.'

England team-mate Joe O'Boye overheard and chirped: 'Well, if we're not playing, we might as well relax and enjoy ourselves.'

He ordered two quadruple vodka and oranges. White said 'Cheers' and ordered two more.

Three hours of drinking later, White was told by Cottier: 'You're on. You're playing against Wales.'

White wrote in his autobiography, *Behind the White Ball*, 'Too stunned to talk, almost too drunk to move, I gazed at him through bleary eyes and seized hold of the bar so I wouldn't fall down.'

Somehow, White was able to piece together a break of 59 'before collapsing to the floor like a sack of potatoes'.

White collapsed again after missing a red and, unsurprisingly, went on to lose 3-0 to Steve Newbury.

After the match, White said Cottier 'came storming up and told me I was a disgrace. From my position on the floor, among the cigarette stubs and beer bottle tops, I gave him a bit of the verbals.

'"That's it, you're not going to Tasmania [for the World Amateur Championships] now – you're out," he snapped, leaving me to stagger to my chalet, where I fell across the bed and passed out, still fully clothed.'

As it turned out, he did go to Tasmania – after paying a £200 fine – and was reunited with O'Boye.

'FAME AND FORTUNE ahead for Joe O'Boye' predicted the *Leicester Mercury* headline in April 1980.

Only 20 years old, O'Boye, whose parents were from Ireland, had just won the English Amateur Snooker Championship in Milton Keynes with a shock win over Dave Martin in the final.

O'Boye, another who served his snooker apprenticeship at Osborne's in Leicester city centre in between shifts on the market, won 13-9 after getting lost when trying to find the venue on the opening day.

O'Boye and White shared the same mischievous streak and somehow or other, they convinced the England team manager to hand over their £1,500 allowance for the World Amateur Championship in advance.

It was a mistake. The moment White and O'Boye landed in Australia they headed to the local racetrack and by the end of the day, their money had gone.

Drunk, they found their way back to the hotel and the team's management threatened to send them home. They decided against that and White went on to win the tournament.

BBC VIEWERS were told they would see 'a left-handed version of Higgins' at the 1981 World Championships.

David Vine was talking about Jimmy White, an 18-year-old from south London who wore a ring in his left ear, played fast and loved Higgins.

'I first played Alex in an exhibition when I was 13,' White remembered.

'He came to a working men's club in Balham, which my dad ran, and tried to chat my sister up. So my brother wanted to knock him out. It was the most horrendous first meeting with your hero ever. I should've known.'

By then White had already made several century breaks and much to the delight of the locals, beat Higgins in the frame they played.

The following weekend, Higgins invited White to an exhibition in Southend.

White proved to be a match for the professionals and on his World Championship debut, he stayed in touch with tournament favourite Davis in their first-round clash until Davis pulled way to win 10-8.

Harvey Lisberg liked the look of White and reckoned that with a few tweaks, he could turn a character he likened to the Artful Dodger, from Charles Dickens's *Oliver Twist*, into a millionaire.

Lisberg owned half of Kennedy Street Enterprises, one of the biggest show business agents in Europe who had pop titans such as ABBA, Queen, Meatloaf and more on their books.

He made his breakthrough spotting Herman's Hermits and saw similar potential in White.

'He's going to look better,' Lisberg was filmed saying after adding White to his stable. 'They all look the same. They all look like penguins.'

The cameras captured Lisberg thinking over a punk hairstyle for White, but he settled for capping his teeth and working on his hair.

Lisberg could sort out White's image, but he couldn't do anything about the way he lived.

White said: 'He [Lisberg] kept saying to me: "You've got to slow down." I was laughing, thinking: "What are you talking about?" He managed rock stars. I thought it was normal.'

The bosses at the Pontin's holiday camp where White stayed during 1981 didn't think his behaviour was 'normal' and told the World Professional Billiards and Snooker Association about it in a letter.

It read: 'At approximately 1.00am, Mr Jimmy White, who was obviously very much the worse for wear for alcohol, was seen by our night cleaning supervisor and a security officer to throw a pint pot up in the air, hitting the ceiling, in a relatively crowded area.

'I was summoned, to find Mr White surrounded by a very young and boisterous group of followers. I attempted to speak to Mr White about the incident, but he was in no condition to listen and walked away. When a more sensible member of his party tried to remonstrate with him, saying that his behaviour might lead to him being banned from Pontins, his comment was: "I don't fucking care."'

Worse was to follow when White was arrested and accused of stealing a handbag during riots in the summer of 1981.

Rioters were sentenced to around three to four months in prison and White would surely receive the same punishment if found guilty.

That was the speculation during the Langs Supreme Scottish Masters in Glasgow.

White had been due to appear in court during the tournament at Kelvin Hall, but his solicitor ensured he was cleared to play and somehow, he was able to hand Steve Davis his first tournament defeat for around 12 months and then beat Cliff Thorburn in the final.

White was then cleared of any wrongdoing during the riots in court, telling the press afterwards: 'It's crazy that you can't walk along the street, see something on the pavement and pick it up out of curiosity without being arrested.'

White was wanted by fans – rather than the police – after a shock 10-4 win over Cliff Thorburn in the first round of the 1982 World Championship.

The trouble was, so little time did White spend at school he struggled to sign the autographs he was constantly being asked for.

Friends would whisper the letters he should write down in his ear. Fans would walk away reading the words: 'You are ugly, sod off, Jimmy White.'

The fairy tale ended in the semi-finals when Higgins pulled off his great escape, an experience that cemented the bond between them.

White and Higgins spent a day at a golf club together and the bill they were presented with the following day became the stuff of legend.

It read: 'Hire of clubs: £20 each. Dinner: £60 each. Two packs of cards: £15. Drinks: £1,100.'

White said later: 'I'm not sure how we managed that. Good night, though. What I can remember of it.'

White liked a drink. He once estimated he drank for 12 consecutive days, admitting to *The Sunday Times*: 'With the lifestyle I had, looking back, I'm surprised I cued up, let alone potted any balls because I wasn't prepared.

'They [his opponents] would have seen me coming in at breakfast and rubbed their hands. "He has been out all night."'

White had other distractions, as manager Geoff Lomas remembered.

He told the papers: 'Jimmy's attractive to women. They all want to mother him – he'd sooner be out with the lads than chatting up a gorgeous girl.

'The proof of that came one night when Jimmy, out with some pals at Bootleggers, the West End nightclub, actually snubbed the one lady most men would love to get to know better, Samantha Fox [who was often pictured posing topless on Page Three of the daily tabloid press].

'Sam would have been quite happy to join Jimmy and his crowd. But instead of leaping at the chance to welcome the Page Three beauty into his circle, Jimmy indicated he just wasn't interested.'

SNOOKER DIDN'T want Joe O'Boye, White's former team-mate and drinking partner.

'You couldn't just turn professional in those days,' said his former manager, Reg Warland.

'It was like a gentlemen's club and you needed a professional player to back you.

'Joe wasn't what they were looking for. They didn't want this Irish upstart.

'They knew he smoked pot, drank and was a bit of a rebel. Everyone knew what he was doing. He would smoke pot and drink in front of people.

'I went up to Ray Reardon once and asked him to vote for Joe and he just looked at me and then walked off. Joe had probably been half-pissed the night before and upset him. While Steve Davis was practising seven or eight hours every day, Joe was getting pissed.'

O'Boye decided against trying to turn professional after winning the English Amateur Championship in 1980 and instead 'spent a couple of years playing money matches', according to Warland.

'Joe had crooks and gamblers backing him. He got in with the wrong people.'

O'Boye got the chance to fulfil his potential after Warland landed a job working for Gordon Banks Promotions, set up by the 1966 World Cup-winning goalkeeper.

'I told them: "There's this kid called Joe O'Boye. He's a bit reckless and headstrong, but he's got loads of potential,"' remembered Warland.

'They asked me to take him on. They said they knew everybody and could get Joe in [to the professional snooker ranks].'

All O'Boye had to do was prove he was good enough – and behave himself.

Warland and O'Boye went on the amateur circuit together and to Warland's frustration, O'Boye drank and smoked away his chance.

'Joe has a bunch of idiots following him,' said Warland. 'They would distract him, encourage him to drink and smoke. I couldn't tell them to get lost, they would have punched my head in, and Joe would tell me: "Don't tell me who I can and can't be friends with."

'Eventually, he agreed with me and said: "I want to get out of Leicester." We travelled to Birmingham to practice with Graham Miles.'

O'Boye's form didn't improve.

'Joe just didn't get any results,' said Warland. 'Every time he got knocked out in the first and second rounds. He was making excuses, but he was smoking a bit of pot and drinking and I tried to get him to stop.

'He would say to me, "Fuck it, you drink," but all I did was have a couple of pints while he was practising all day. I said: "That doesn't affect you."

'We would argue every single day.

'Joe wasn't really a massive drinker, but he didn't handle it very well. He would change personality after he had a drink and start being belligerent and stupid.'

There was a fall-out with room-mate Mike Hallett after O'Boye threw some of his possessions out of a hotel window and Warland remembers him 'going berserk' after he was barred from a club in Birmingham.

'Joe had a big match the following day,' remembered Warland, 'and he said he was going to his room for a quiet night.

'A few of us went to the Rum Runner and there was suddenly a ruckus at the door.

'Joe had turned up and they told him he was barred. The night before he had sprayed someone behind the bar with a soda syphon and they had chucked him out.

'Someone told him, "Your manager's in there," and he went berserk when he saw I was in there drinking.

'They got him out, but he was weird with me for days after that.'

O'Boye's form on the table was also puzzling.

'He kept losing to people who he was better than,' said Warland.

'He should have had the pride to say to himself: "I'm not letting these mugs beat me," but he used to throw matches away on purpose.

'I think winning the English Amateur title made Joe think he was better than he was and when he didn't get the results he wanted, he couldn't handle it.

'Joe was very good in the balls. When he got close to the balls he was fast and exciting. He could put together a break of 50 or 60 in no time at all, but his safety game was very poor and his long potting was suspect. I tried to talk to him, but he didn't have the patience. He would say, "I'm not taking 45 minutes to win a frame of snooker." He wanted to win it in one or two visits and sometimes he did, but then he would lose the next three frames by choosing the wrong shot.

'I didn't think his heart was in it. He got bored. He didn't understand why some players got to 28 on a break and then played safe. The amateur circuit was tough and every single player was playing to win. That wasn't Joe's style. He wanted to be exciting all the time and he couldn't adapt. He was so gung-ho. He just didn't seem to have the will to grind out a result and then he stopped turning up for practice.

'The managing director of the promotions company was putting me under pressure. I was telling Joe, "You're going to get the sack."'

O'Boye finally found some form, reaching the quarter-finals of a tournament. He faced Robert Marshall in a match that went to a deciding black ball.

'Marshall played a safety shot and the obvious shot was a double across the table, leaving the white ball safe on the bottom cushion,' remembered Warland.

'There was no way you could cut the black into the middle pocket.

'Joe could see I was watching intently and when he went down on the shot, he looked up at me and winked. Then he did it again.

'He played the shot at 100 miles per hour – and missed the black completely.

'He just didn't care. He was trying to wind me up.

'He was his own worst enemy. The shot he tried was a one-in-a-thousand shot. It was the most ridiculous shot I've ever seen.

'It was so obvious that he should have gone for the double and even Marshall said to me afterwards: "What the fuck was he doing? If he had missed the double he would have left it safe."

'I was infuriated and stormed off into the lounge. I said to him: "That's the worst shot I've ever seen you play."'

O'Boye answered: 'You're the worst manager I've ever had.'

'I'm the only manager you've ever had.'

Warland remembers them 'falling about laughing, but it was serious. My job was on the line.'

Warland lost his job and O'Boye lost his backing.

O'Boye did eventually knuckle down and, at the fourth attempt, he was granted his professional licence by the WPBSA, in the summer of 1984.

O'BOYE AND WHITE were reunited at the 1985 Rothman's Grand Prix in Reading.

They were drawn against each other in the last 32.

The match would be O'Boye's television debut and he left an impression on those watching.

By then, O'Boye was living in Bristol and on the day of the match, he caught the train to Reading – eventually.

The train was delayed and O'Boye arrived at the Hexagon Theatre only 15 minutes before the best-of-nine-frames match was due to start.

O'Boye would need to get changed into his suit quickly, but he couldn't find it.

Though the suit had been delivered to the venue two days earlier, O'Boye didn't know where it was and, with time running out, O'Boye was still in his underwear, in a state of panic.

White offered to lend O'Boye an outfit, but with the start of the match only five minutes away, he found his suit.

O'Boye started the match with a miscued break that gifted White four points, but put that horror start behind him to open up a shock 4-2 lead. That left him one frame away from winning the match and O'Boye had his chances in the seventh frame. He missed them and White nudged him out 5-4, saying afterwards: 'Joe should have beaten me.

'He had his chances in that seventh frame, but he seemed to rush his shots.'

O'Boye told the press afterwards: 'I can't tell you all the things that happened to me today. It's too long a story, but certainly all the messing about before the start didn't help.'

Tony Knowles offered his opinion of what happened to O'Boye, saying: 'The finishing line's in sight and there's a fear of bursting it.'

O'Boye played well enough to stop Alex Higgins reaching the final of the Irish Professional Championship, in 1988, but is best remembered for being on the receiving end of a record-breaking thrashing ...

EVERY SNOOKER fan knows 'The Whirlwind,' 'The Rocket' and 'The Hurricane'.

'They were nowhere near as quick as me,' says 'The Tornado'.

Tony Drago was 'The Tornado' from Malta, explaining: 'I'm a very hyperactive and nervous character on and off the table and that's why I play fast.

'If I go to buy a pair of shoes and there are ten people in front of me in the queue, I go home and come back the next day.

'People have tried to give me advice on my technique and I stop them. I never listened to any of them. I play the game the way I've always played the game.'

O'Boye had a similar attitude to Drago, but he was no match for him when they met in the 1990 UK Championship in Preston.

'YOU CAN'T BUY YOUTH'

Drago whitewashed O'Boye 9-0 in just 81 minutes, an average of nine minutes per frame.

That was the fastest best-of-17-frames match recorded in a professional tournament.

O'Boye, who made his sole World Championship appearance at the Crucible in 1989 and was beaten by Silvino Francisco, had his problems going into the match. He was in trouble for swearing at an official during the Grand Prix in Reading a few weeks earlier, an outburst that earned him a ban from the 1991 Mercantile Credit Classic and World Championship.

'I don't regret anything,' said O'Boye defiantly when asked about his failure to live up to his early promise. 'You're only young once and you can't buy youth.'

COCAINE KIRK AND THE CANADIANS

'WHEN I was 15, I looked like 12,' remembered Kirk Stevens.

'So when this little wimp went up to somebody and said, "Like to play for $500?" they thought they couldn't lose.'

Stevens wasn't quite that bold when he first approached Cliff Thorburn at a club in Toronto.

'I was the pro,' said Cliff, 'and Kirk's family didn't live far away. He asked me to play him for $2 a game.

'I beat him a couple of games and he offered to pay me, but I said: "I don't want your money." He made me take the money and a few years later he beat me in the final of the Canadian national championship. Maybe I should have insisted that he kept his money ...'

Stevens spent too much time in pool halls and was kicked out of school when he was 13 years old for persistent truancy. By then, he had started smoking drugs.

Thorburn said there were always drugs available to regulars at pool halls and snooker clubs in Canada. 'A lot of guys sample stuff just for the hell of it and then decide it's bad for them and just don't get involved anymore,' he said.

'Somehow, Kirk got hooked.'

Stevens headed around North America hustling pool where he had more scrapes. 'I was beaten up a couple of times, black eyes and stuff like that,' he remembered.

The snooker circuit in the UK was less dangerous and more appreciative of Stevens's talents.

Commentators said Stevens brought 'Las Vegas-style showmanship' to snooker.

'Kirk was like a breath of fresh air,' said Thorburn. 'He spread the balls more than Alex ever did. Alex would play around the pack, but Kirk was more aggressive. He would bust the balls open early.'

Stevens didn't even have to strike the cue ball to get the audience's attention.

Snooker Scene described his attire at the 1981 Langs Supreme Scottish Masters as 'tight black leather trousers, white waistcoat, black collarless shirt with most of the buttons undone and white shoes with flapping laces which could have graced a tennis court'.

He was best known for wearing a white outfit that drew comparisons to John Travolta's character in the film *Saturday Night Fever*, described by snooker journalist Dave Hendon as 'another icon of the era'.

'You should have heard the gasps when I walked into the room,' he said when remembering the reaction to his white suit.

Thorburn said this showmanship was used to cure Stevens's shyness.

'Kirk was shy,' he said. 'He ran around the table wearing a white suit – and that's no way to lower your profile! But he didn't really like to play in front of big crowds. I only found that out years later.'

Shy or not, Stevens could play snooker.

He first came to the attention of *Snooker Scene* when, as an 18-year-old, he was beaten by Alex Higgins in the 1976 Canadian Open, the magazine reporting Stevens 'was not overawed when playing Higgins and played nearly as fast as he did'. Stevens endured tragedy while still in his teens. 'I had just turned 19, and like any normal teenager I had been out to a disco in downtown Toronto,' he remembered.

'I was living at the time with my dad and older sister, Robin.

'My parents had split up when I was seven and my mum lived with my other sister, Cory, and my brother, Jack Junior, just three miles away.

'We all saw a lot of each other and I remember thinking I would go and stay at my mum's house that night. For some reason, I decided to stop off at our place on the way over there. It was then that I heard that my mum had been killed in a house fire.

'I rushed over there, but there was nothing I could do. My brother and sister got out alive after being woken by the dog, but my mother didn't make it.

'Apparently, she had a few drinks earlier in the evening and I guess she didn't wake up when the dog started barking.

'My bitter resignation turned to vengeful fury when my girlfriend, Jenny, phoned me in the early hours to tell me she had had a menacing anonymous call.

'She told me a man had rang her and threatened: "You're next."'

The police confirmed Stevens's mother was the victim of an arson attack.

He said: 'I was in the mood to kill. Every night for weeks after I used to go over to my girl's place and lie in wait with a gun, hoping these guys would show up.

'I had an old Winchester rifle and I was ready to use it. I used to hide in some thick bushes by her garage with my finger on the trigger, but no one ever appeared.'

He threw himself into snooker and *Snooker Scene* reported on the 'young, brash potter' making his way through the qualifiers for the 1979 World Championship.

The following year, aged just 21, Stevens became the youngest player to reach the semi-finals of the sport's premier tournament, knocking out John Spencer and Eddie Charlton on the way to the last four, where he was beaten by Higgins.

Stevens invested some of his winnings in a plush London flat where the tabloids reported he lived a 'wild' life.

'There is never any shortage of pretty girls whenever Kirk Stevens is around,' started a Press Association feature.

'They clamour for his autograph, shower him with gifts – and frequently inundate him with sexy invitations.'

Stevens enjoyed himself rather too much and after his form dipped, Mike Watterson, the promoter who took the World Championship to the Crucible Theatre, invited Stevens to stay with him at his Chesterfield home, where there were fewer distractions.

JIMMY WHITE was the player who brought the best out of Stevens. They lived the same way – and played snooker the same way. Fast.

Stevens was popping champagne corks after their match in the Benson & Hedges Masters in 1984 – despite losing.

In the ninth frame, Stevens became only the third player, after Steve Davis and Thorburn, to make a maximum 147 break in a major televised tournament.

It took him 12 minutes and 57 seconds to pot 15 reds, 15 blacks and all the colours and Thorburn was there to see him do it.

He said: 'I was in the green room backstage with [Canadian actor] Donald Sutherland.

'We were talking and I asked him if he wanted to go inside to watch because he had never seen a frame of snooker before.

'He sat there with his overcoat on his lap, watched Kirk make his 147 and then left because he had to be somewhere else!

'That was the one frame of snooker he saw in his life.'

Bizarrely, a representative of the sponsors stepped out of the audience after Stevens completed his 147 break to give him a £10 note, saying it was a down payment on the £10,000 bonus for his maximum.

The break reduced White's lead to 5-4 in the best-of-11-frames match and White's response was breathtaking.

He won the match with a break of 119, providing a jaw-dropping finish to an extraordinary duel with a pair of 'banana shots' on the final pink and black, sending the cue ball curving crazily around the table to gasps from the audience. Stevens smiled along with them.

Five weeks later, Stevens almost topped his 147, at the Yamaha International Masters in Derby.

Mike Watterson, Stevens' former landlord, fouled on the yellow with his opening shot, handing Stevens a free ball.

He took the brown with the free ball, meaning that with 15 reds still on the table, a break of 152 was possible.

Stevens took blacks with his first 11 reds and then ran out of position. He knocked in pinks after the 12th and 13th reds, leaving a possible break of 150, but he missed the 14th red, the break ending on 107.

COCAINE KIRK AND THE CANADIANS

'SURE, THERE are girls,' Stevens told the Press Association in a feature penned in February 1984.

'And I like to have relationships with them. But it's for now, only casual.

'I make that clear, otherwise it wouldn't be fair.'

Stevens was ranked No. 7 in the world at the time and fancied he would be crowned world champion in a few weeks.

The only player he thought could stop him was White.

The 22-year-old was making his last attempt to become the youngest to win the World Championship and he faced Stevens in the semi-finals.

Stevens said: 'I decided to take Jimmy on at his own game and go for my shots.'

Neither player was well. Stevens was struggling with tonsillitis, while White had a stomach bug that forced him to leave the arena to be sick at one point.

They still produced one of the greatest games ever seen at the Crucible.

Stevens went from 5-1 down to lead 12-10 going into the final session of the best-of-31-frames match.

White missed a long red early in the 23rd frame, leaving commentator Ted Lowe to sigh: 'That's the style of Jimmy White; either they go down or you let your opponent in.'

Stevens cashed in to make 52 before missing a pink. White could still win the frame, but with the pink and black unpottable, he had work to do.

White's first shot sent a red into each of the bottom corner pockets and freed the pink and black. The break reached 33 before White snookered himself on the last red. His successful escape left the red within Stevens' range. He knocked it in to take his lead to 21 points, but didn't get position on a colour and rolled the cue ball on to the bottom cushion under the black spot, with the yellow on its spot.

White thought about his next shot, for a second or two. The yellow was barely a half-chance, but if he sank it, White would surely clean up the colours and trail by only one frame. Miss and he could be 13-10 down.

White slammed the yellow into its pocket and mopped up the remaining five colours. Stevens had thrown the frame away and worse was to follow for him as White turned his 12-10 deficit into a 15-12 lead.

White went on to win a classic match 16-14, leaving referee Jim Thorpe to say: 'I've never seen snooker like it. From one player, perhaps, but never two at the same time. It was like table tennis on a billiard table as the balls flew down from every angle.'

The final between White and Davis was just as absorbing. From 12-4 behind, White fought back and had chances to force a deciding 35th frame, but a rush of blood to his head on the green in the 34th gifted Davis a straightforward opening.

'The Whirlwind' didn't take defeat well.

He revealed in his autobiography that the loss sent him on a three-month crack cocaine spree.

That included a binge with Stevens during the Irish Masters.

White described Stevens as 'a big cocaine taker on the snooker circuit' and remembered begging guests at the Keaden Hotel in County Kildare for lighters so he could cook the drug.

'Some must have guessed I was an addict by then because I looked awful,' he wrote.

'I ran back, emptied my pockets and spilled these lighters all over his bed.

'[Kirk] had rocks on him so we started trying to cook them.

'I started trying to dismantle the door of the wardrobe so we could use it as firewood.

'We started breaking down the furniture in the room, a table here, a wardrobe there, trying to get a fire started so we could cook this stuff up.

'That's how sadistic the drug is, that's how crazy it had sent us. Two of the best snooker players in the world, holed away in an Irish hotel room, smashing up chairs and ripping up a duvet so we could make an indoor fire and smoke some crack.'

White said he 'couldn't handle' seeing his wife Maureen when she called to the hotel room the next day.

'I ran upstairs to my room and tried to hide,' he said.

'She walked in and was about to go off on one at me. She started screaming, "Jimmy, where the hell have you been?"

'She tried to sit down on this vanity stool. Unfortunately for her, me and Kirk had tried to burn the legs off it the night before.

'The legs gave way and she fell to the floor. We all burst into laughter. That broke the ice and I got away with it.'

THIS MAYHEM happened during what Stevens described as a five-month break from the game.

Clive Everton soberly wrote that during that period, Stevens had 'too many late nights'.

On his return to the circuit, Stevens made first-round exits from his next three tournaments before he went to stay with John Virgo and his wife and set about rebuilding his game.

Stevens decided to model his game on Steve Davis and they met each other in the semi-finals of the Dulux British Open in Derby in March 1985.

The best-of-17-frames match turned into an eight-and-a-half-hour grind.

Usually, this would have suited Davis, but he found Stevens was more than his equal on this occasion, the Canadian coming out on top 9-7 after a match that finished past midnight.

In the final he met Silvino Francisco, a South African who was also appearing in his first major ranking final.

Francisco, whose dark good looks earned him many female admirers, had been considered a good prospect for years, having started playing as a boy.

Manuel Francisco had sold two fishing boats to help buy a restaurant and shop that had two billiard tables, much to the fascination of his nine-year-old son, Silvino.

Silvino and elder brother Manuel dominated the South African Billiards Championship, lifting the trophy 14 times in 15 years between them, and when they played each other in the 1976 World Amateur Snooker Championships, Silvino won on his way to the semi-finals.

He knew a good run at the British Open would take him into the top 16 of the world rankings for the first time and in the semi-finals, he faced Higgins.

There was controversy, as there often was once 'The Hurricane' started to lose.

A couple of spectators were asked to leave for shouting out during the match and there was a flashpoint in the 11th frame when there was a dispute over a free ball. Francisco was the beneficiary and went on to win 9-6.

Manager Geoff Lomas once said that Higgins never genuinely lost a match fair and square, that someone else was always to blame, and this was no exception.

Higgins blamed the audience and referee John Williams.

He said: 'The audience was so flat. The audience looked like they were on Valium and I couldn't raise a gallop.'

As for the disputed free ball, Higgins said: 'I'm going to insist that referees take regular eye tests.'

Francisco–Stevens was the first ranking final to be played out by non-British players, but that is not how the match is remembered.

After the second session, Francisco made a complaint to tournament director Paul Hatherell. He apparently felt the Canadian was playing under the influence of drugs. Hatherell took no action against Stevens, but during the final day, Francisco confronted the Canadian in the toilets.

News of this altercation reached newspaper reporter Neil Wallis after Francisco had won the match 12-9 and he followed up the story by visiting Francisco's home.

Sections of the interview were recorded and Wallis made notes on the rest of what Francisco told him for a story that appeared on the front page of the *Daily Star* on the opening day of the 1985 World Championship.

Francisco was quoted as saying Stevens was 'as high as a kite, out of his mind on dope'.

Francisco denied making the comments. He said the story was '95 per cent' untrue when facing the press after losing 10-2 to Dennis Taylor in the opening round.

He told them: 'I might have said something to Kirk, but I don't know what it was. You get in quite a state during a final.'

Francisco added: 'I have no evidence of drug-taking during matches and I've never felt I've played against anyone who had taken drugs.'

The WPBSA fined Francisco £6,000 and docked him two ranking points for 'bringing the game into disrepute'.

Two weeks after Francisco's claims were published, Stevens told the paper his side of things and it proved to be the same story.

Stevens said he had been hooked on cocaine since he was 19 years old, spending an estimated $200 every day on the drug.

He said: 'I think I've probably wasted about $250,000, possibly more, on this drug over the last six years or so.'

He went into a clinic in Canada in a bid to cure his addiction and in October 1985, the WPBSA decided at a meeting at a hotel in Stoke to take no action against the world No. 5.

The following month, Stevens was on a life support machine in St Stephen's Hospital in Fulham.

The Sun newspaper reported he was in a 'cocaine coma' and once Stevens had been discharged, publicist Max Clifford said the incident had 'nothing whatsoever to do with drugs. It was a blockage of the lungs which caused breathing problems'.

Stevens's behaviour had been erratic, however. The WPBSA had been unhappy with him after he had failed to turn up to the Irish Masters earlier that year.

They accepted his explanation that he had simply missed his plane and fined him £500.

There had been other instances of Stevens failing to turn up for tournaments, notably the Jameson International Open, and the tabloids went looking for stories.

'Smokey' Joe Thickett was happy to talk to them. He described himself as a drug dealer who knew a few of the top snooker players, including Stevens.

Thickett said: 'He [Stevens] knew all about cocaine long before he came to England. When we were introduced, he said: "Smokey Joe? I'm Cocaine Kirk."

'Once he arrived at my home after flying in from Canada. He put his cue up against a wall and went on a solid, three-day binge.

'Finally, Kirk crashed out on my carpet and just slept and slept ... I was staggered at the way he put away gram after gram.'

Manager Geoff Lomas denied Stevens was under the influence during the Dulux British Open, but admitted he was close to death days before the tournament began.

He told the press: 'It was the night, just before the Dulux Open, that he nearly overdosed on cocaine and whisky.

'He had woken me in the early hours to say he was going back to Canada – then and there.

'I went into the kitchen to make coffee and saw some white powder on the floor. Cocaine.

'Kirk had staggered downstairs and, before I could stop him, filled a tumbler with Canadian Club whisky and gulped it down in one.

'He began to shake and make strange gargling noises. I was frightened. I thought he was dying.

'I dragged him into the toilet and stuck my fingers down his throat to make him sick. Then I carried him into the garden and, supporting his weight, walked him round and round, for literally hours.'

Though his life was saved, Stevens's snooker career soon looked to be over.

He failed to win a televised match throughout the 1987/88 season, a run that led to him dropping out of the top 32, and when interviewed in 1989, Stevens had managed to hitch a lift to the European Championship in France, only to be beaten in his first match.

Then there was a £50,000 tax bill that needed paying, along with his £350 monthly rent.

'Me and Steve Davis turned pro at the same meeting,' he laughed. 'Reflect on those two careers …'

Stevens knew his lifestyle was to blame and said his cocaine addiction cost him more than his career. 'After a while you become impotent,' he revealed. 'Frightening, isn't it? Impotent in your twenties. Just another bloody thing the White Lady does.

'If I had a good girl, she could only hang on for so long. But, sure, I couldn't believe how many girls passed me by. But I soon grew into the idea that I didn't want to go to bed with anybody I didn't want to wake up with.'

Stevens said crack cocaine 'sucked everything out of me. It's the worst stuff in the world.

'If there was a poll taken now: "Kirk Stevens, what do they remember me for?" I bet you, dollars to doughnuts, it wouldn't be for my fine snooker playing.'

Stevens kept losing and days after a defeat to John Parrott at the 1992 UK Championships, he was declared bankrupt and decided to head home.

He would later say: 'I had no heart for the game.'

Thorburn said: 'Between 1980 and 1984, Kirk was good enough to win the World Championship. He had the tools to win it and was pretty focused. There's a reason why he didn't win it. He either lacked a bit extra or there were other people around …'

There were stories that after his return to Canada, Stevens worked behind the counter at the club where he had first played as a boy.

He was also rumoured to work in construction, as a car salesman and as a gardener.

Stevens had a rethink one day in 1996, saying: 'I was 60 feet up a tree, holding a chainsaw. I was just about to start cutting when I realised I'd got to guess how the damn thing would fall to jump out of the way. Snooker suddenly didn't seem so bad again.'

He went on to win the North American qualifier in 1998 to regain his professional status and there was plenty of press interest when Stevens returned to the circuit later that year, playing in a qualifier in Plymouth.

His opening match was against the world No. 114 Ian Sargeant, a Welshman who, as a 14-year-old, had watched Stevens play White in the 1984 World Championship semi-final and thought it was the best match he had ever seen.

His match with Stevens wouldn't hit such heights. Stevens started the best-of-nine-frames match – and saw the cue ball disappear into a corner pocket from the break.

Martin Johnson, reporting on the match for the *Daily Telegraph*, wrote: 'It was one of those matches in which the players matched each other not so much pot for pot, as miss for miss.'

Stevens missed more than Sargeant and was beaten 5-2 after collecting just 46 points in the final four frames.

He made the breezy admission that he had 'played awful' before adding: 'It's just fantastic to be involved again. I'm lucky to have lived this long. Life can be tricky – especially when you get carried away like I did.'

Stevens said it would take time to get used to the speed of the tables and joked, 'I think they've shaved a bit off the pockets as well,' but there was to be no return to the snooker elite, saying the attention he received was partly to blame.

'It was embarrassing, being on the front pages all the time and I was just exhausted from fighting all the shit, the perceptions people had about me,' he told *The Observer* in 2002.

'I didn't say goodbye to anyone ... I just wanted to come home ...'

Stevens did return to Britain in 2011.

He was invited to take part in a Snooker Legends night held at the Crucible Theatre and faced White, 27 years after their epic World Championship semi-final.

To the delight of the crowd, the single frame was played in the same spirit as their classic clashes.

The white waistcoat was a rather tighter fit around Stevens, but, as he always did, he went for absolutely everything when at the table.

He pulled off a spectacular double that brought gasps from the audience and once among the balls, Stevens was able to make a break of 45 that was enough to win him the frame.

THE MOST successful Canadian player was described as 'an Edwardian gentleman' by Jimmy White.

Even an 'Edwardian gentleman' has a breaking point ...

Cliff Thorburn was born in Victoria, British Columbia in Canada and abandoned by his mother when he was only 18 months old.

He spent time in an orphanage until it was agreed his father and grandmother would look after him.

Cliff was told his mother had died and says discovering the truth gave him added determination to succeed.

Aged 12, Thorburn went to a bowling alley with his father and after heading downstairs, he heard the click of pool balls coming from a room. Intrigued, he went to see what was happening and saw that a crowd had gathered to watch a pool match.

'Then all this money suddenly appeared on the table,' he said. 'Then someone spotted me. The guy yelled at me, "Get outta here, kid," and I scrambled back up the stairs.'

As a teenager, Thorburn started playing pool himself and by the age of 16 he was a regular at the Cue and Cushion club in Victoria.

He would save up the money he earned by emptying bins to use as stake money.

'I was playing this guy for some money – not a huge amount – with some guys watching,' remembered Thorburn.

'My dad came to the top of the stairs and shouted down: "Don't play snooker."

'Soon as he said that, I started practising five hours a day instead of one. He said: "Listen son, the snooker is really starting to get in the way of your schoolwork." So I quit school. I wasn't very clever with my decisions then.'

Thorburn would hitch-hike around North America playing money matches knowing that should he lose, he would not be able to afford any overnight accommodation.

He took on characters such as 'Oil Can' Harry and 'Suitcase' Sam and usually, he won.

There was a confrontation after a match against a fisherman in Campbell River, British Columbia.

'Are you hustling me?' the fisherman asked Thorburn angrily.

'No, sir,' replied Thorburn and the fisherman pulled back his coat to reveal a large fishing knife attached to his belt.

He patted the sheath with his hand and asked again: 'Are you hustling me?'

The bartender saw the danger and grabbed the fisherman's hand to defuse the situation.

Thorburn said he never hustled; he always played his best game.

On one occasion Thorburn gave an opponent a 70-point start in a snooker frame and only played with the rest.

He still won.

'There wasn't a lot of American pool [in Canada],' said Thorburn.

'There was a lot of gambling on snooker matches and variations of snooker. They would put numbered balls on the snooker table and play it like pool. It was rough and tough.'

As his reputation grew and his photograph appeared in a magazine, Thorburn had to disguise himself to get matches.

He was introduced to snooker when Fred Davis and Rex Williams visited Canada and he headed to Britain in 1973 after John Spencer gave him a vote of confidence.

'I played John Spencer in 1972 and asked if he thought I was good enough to turn professional,' said Thorburn. 'He said I was.'

The Thorburn who arrived in Britain in 1973 had a rather different look.

He had the 'Afro' haircut that was a legacy of the drugs scene in North America and said that on his first day in Britain, he ran into Higgins.

Higgins offered him a 40-point start for £5 per frame.

'Being the gentleman I am, I only took 28,' said Thorburn. 'I don't think Alex won a game.

'All I remember is Higgins at the top of some stairs, I still haven't been paid and he's got a ball in his hand, threatening to throw it at me.'

Months later, Thorburn and Higgins came to blows after a game of cards. 'Higgins went broke and asked me to lend him £50,' remembered Thorburn.

'I'm losing as well, so I say OK, if he gives me his ring. He's with Cara, his first wife, so that night she comes down to my room and demands the ring off me.

'I say "No," so Alex pretended to faint on the floor. I went to pick him up and the guy grabbed a bottle. I got my left hand around him and just pounded him until my hand got sore.'

There was friction when they met in the final of the 1980 World Championship.

Higgins accused Thorburn of standing in his line of vision when he was playing; Thorburn said Higgins was clinking his glass as he took aim.

With the scores tied at 16-16, Lynn Higgins, Alex's wife, went into the players' room carrying a cake decorated with the words: 'Congratulations, year of The Hurricane. Alex Higgins, World Champion, 1980.'

Thorburn recalled with a smile that he had six slices of the cake after winning 18-16.

Thorburn was nicknamed 'The Grinder' by Higgins in recognition of his steely determination to win.

Though respected for his hardness, Thorburn wasn't loved the way Higgins was.

For the public, Higgins was the star and when they played exhibitions together, even when Thorburn was the world champion, Higgins was paid more.

There was further trouble between Thorburn and Higgins at the Langs Scottish Masters later in 1981.

Higgins noticed the score was wrong during a frame.

'Alex knows the rules,' wrote Thorburn in his autobiography. 'You're taken to have condoned any mistake if you play on, which he had. There was no check scorer and the referee had called the score wrong' but that was not the point. Alex made a big fuss, called me a cheat when it was over and tried to talk the organisers into playing the match over again.'

Thorburn went to his hotel room and the phone rang. It was Higgins. 'I hope to hell your son doesn't grow up to be like you.'

Thorburn's son, Jamie, had been born three months earlier. On that occasion, Thorburn decided not to confront Higgins, but when they bumped into each other after playing in the Irish Masters, Thorburn couldn't keep his hands off him.

Higgins had overturned a 4-0 deficit to win their match 5-4 and told Thorburn in the bar afterwards: 'You're a Canadian @@@@ and you can't fucking play either.'

Thorburn remembered: 'This was too much. He walked over to me and I'm so mad I just hit him. Not quite on the chin, more like his jaw to the side. He's gone down.

'Some of his friends grabbed him; some other people grabbed me. Some drunk says: "Let's all be friends." As we go to shake hands, I kick him right in the nuts.'

To the public, Thorburn was a dignified character. So clean-cut was his image, he advertised washing machines in women's magazines.

There was friction between Higgins and Thorburn – again – following their match at the 1986 Scottish Masters.

The players rowed over whether Higgins had hit a blue and after losing the match, Higgins confronted Thorburn in the sponsors' room.

'You're lucky,' seethed Higgins.

'Why's that?'

'You know, the bags of white powder.'

The accusation was accurate.

Thorburn tested positive for cocaine during the British Open in February 1988.

Hearn, his manager at the time, got a court injunction that enabled Thorburn to play at the World Championship where he reached the semi-finals, losing to Davis.

Davis went on to retain the world title, having beaten Joe Johnson in the final 12 months earlier, and Thorburn was handed a £10,000 fine, docked two ranking points and suspended from the next two tournaments.

'My house was daubed with abuse,' he said, 'and I received two death threats. People forget that I was world No. 1, but they sure remember the scandal.'

That incident would send Thorburn sliding down the rankings. He mused years later: 'I used to live like a millionaire.'

ONE OF Thorburn's contemporaries played a shot that features in lists of the top 10 ever seen on a snooker table.

It came in a match between Bill Werbeniuk and Joe Johnson in the first round of the 1985 World Championship.

Only Werbeniuk knew what he was thinking when he took aim at a red that was obscured by the yellow and another red.

He dug deep into the cue ball, sending it jumping over the yellow and red before connecting with the red at precisely the right angle to send it flying into the bottom corner.

The crowd cheered their approval, while Werbeniuk shrugged his shoulders and smiled to himself.

Werbeniuk knew how to make balls do what he wanted having spent most of his life with a cue in his hand.

He grew up playing in Pop's Billiards, a hall owned by his father, known as 'Shorty' Werbeniuk.

Bill once described him as 'one of the biggest [crooks] in Canada', who 'committed armed robberies, peddled drugs, every larceny in the language'.

By the age of 12, Bill was winning money on matches, often chuckling as he took his winnings.

'He [was] always trying to get his hands in our pockets,' Thorburn recalled.

Thorburn said: 'We both lived in Vancouver in the late 1960s, 1970s and would play money matches against each other.

'One time when neither of us had any money, we played for punches on the arm. I hit Bill too hard after winning a frame and he hit me back so hard I couldn't move my arm or play for a week.

'There's pressure playing for everything you own, but playing Bill for whacks on the arm is really tough.'

There was weight behind Werbeniuk's punches. He scaled as much as 25 stones (160kg).

Werbeniuk was a drinker – and had to be.

Because of a hereditary nervous disorder, his cueing arm would tremble and to settle it, Werbeniuk drank.

To the amusement of the tabloid press, he claimed tax relief for his alcohol consumption.

He said: 'My reputation was such that I was once hired for £500 to go to this pub in Middlesbrough and just drink. No snooker, just to knock back pints all night.'

There was an occasion when Werbeniuk drank competitively, against a fellow snooker player. Twice Scottish champion – at snooker – Eddie Sinclair fancied he could match Werbeniuk pint for pink – and discovered he couldn't.

Legend has it, Sinclair passed out after his 42nd pint, while Werbeniuk polished off his 43rd and said: 'I'm away for a proper drink.'

Werbeniuk followed Thorburn to Britain and turned professional in 1973.

After reaching the quarter-finals of the World Championship in 1978, he decided to stay in Britain.

He bought an old bus for £20,000, furnished it with a television, video, stereo, kitchen, shower, two bedrooms, lounge, telephone and a lager pump and parked it a few hundred metres from the North Midlands Snooker Centre in Worksop, Nottinghamshire.

Danny Fowler was another professional based there and White, Thorburn and Thorne were regular visitors for money matches.

Werbeniuk's practice partners at the North Midlands Snooker Centre included teenager Craig Frost. 'We would clean the table and when Bill had polished off a gallon of booze, we would play!' remembered Frost, who went on to manage the club, by then renamed Breakers.

'He would have at least eight pints before he could play. I remember asking Bill if he was ready to play and him replying: "I just need a couple more pints." When he was ready, he would play for hours. Bill would play anyone and was happy to pass on tips.'

He also loved to entertain and would play the locals one-handed, resting his cue on the cushion and trying to steer the balls into the pockets.

Werbeniuk was at his peak in 1983.

He lost the Lada Classic Final to Davis and went into the World Championship seeded ninth.

He was beaten 13-11 by Higgins in the quarter-finals.

Werbeniuk dropped out of the top 16 at the end of the 1984/85 season after a dip in form and worse was to come.

Because of the damage his drinking was doing to Werbeniuk's heart, doctors prescribed beta blocker Inderal and that was on the WPBSA's list of banned substances.

Werbeniuk protested that Inderal did not enhance performance, just enable it, but snooker bosses stood firm.

Frost remembered: 'Bill couldn't play without drinking or the beta blockers. His hands shook too much.'

Werbeniuk failed to get beyond the qualifying rounds of the World Championship for three successive years.

In his last bid to reach the Crucible, he was beaten 10-1 by Nigel Bond in 1990 and afterwards said: 'I've had 24 pints of extra strong lager and eight double vodkas and I'm still not drunk.'

After that, he disappeared.

'He didn't say goodbye,' remembered Frost. 'He just went. We didn't know if he was going to come back – and he never did.'

Werbeniuk had gone home to Canada where he died in January 2003, aged 56, having spent the last 13 years living on disability benefits.

In 2002, he told the BBC: 'I live with my mother and brother and watch sport on TV. I don't follow the modern game. All the young players are so boring. I have no idea who any of them are.'

THE MELTER

'WHAT YOU do is this, Jim,' Tony Knowles told Jimmy White once when the subject turned to 'pulling birds'.

'Stand in the nightclub at the highest point where all the birds can see you and then at about ten to two, make your way to the bar ...'

White reckoned Knowles' tactic was successful.

'He'd only have about three drinks all night and he was fighting them off,' said White.

It was estimated that, during the sport's boom years, 55 per cent of the millions of viewers were women.

Jean Rafferty explained in *The Cruel Game* that, 'It's the ideal form of revenge for all those years of being excluded from male sport, the perfect game for watching men as sex objects – all that strutting round the table, displaying their elegant ensembles; the bending and stretching that makes clothes cling tightly to sensual bodies; the moments of silence when the light above the table falls fleetingly on to sculpted male cheekbones.'

There was more to it than that. Women journalists sent to write colour pieces on snooker wrote of snooker's combination of gentlemen's club snobbery and the wickedness of a mis-spent youth.

Manager Geoff Lomas reckoned women wanted to 'mother' White, while Cliff Thorburn was compared to Rhett Butler, the character played by Clark Gable in

Hollywood epic *Gone With the Wind* and all the top players had their admirers. Even Bill Werbeniuk was spotted outside the Crucible Theatre on occasions with a woman on each arm.

'The appeal of snooker to women is a lot more subtle than them just watching all the bending and stretching and bottoms up in the air as the men play tricky shots,' wrote Rafferty.

'Far more important than what they look like is how they behave. They're courteous and elegant and they obey the rules of the game without question.'

Tony Knowles got more female attention than most. There was a time in the mid-1980s when Knowles was on the front pages of the tabloid press so often, he was surely one of the most recognisable sportsmen in the country.

But it wasn't his sporting ability that was being written about.

In the same way that Kirk Stevens felt his snooker achievements were largely forgotten, Knowles possibly got more column inches in newspapers for his extracurricular activities than his snooker, though as a snooker player he came close to knocking a peak Steve Davis off the top of the world rankings ...

Knowles' fascination with the sport started after his father got a job as a steward at Tonge Moor Conservative Club when Tony was nine years old.

Tony could play on the pool and snooker tables whenever he wished and said: 'I'd always play the older lads for drinks.

'They'd be on beer, I'd be on pop.

'I remember staggering out carrying three cases of lemonade.'

His interest in the cue sports grew when, as a 14-year-old-boy, he saw Alex Higgins playing in his home town of Bolton, the first time 'The Hurricane' had appeared outside Ireland. He helped Belfast YMCA win the UK Team Trophy and after being handed the trophy by John Pulman, Higgins then beat the former world champion in an exhibition frame.

Higgins was so popular with Bolton audiences he was invited back to play world champion John Spencer in exhibition matches – and every ticket was sold.

THE WORLD Professional Billiards and Snooker Association didn't like the look of Tony Knowles.

Twice they rejected his bid to become a professional. Though he won the UK Junior Championship in 1972 and 1974 during a good amateur career, there were objections. Knowles hadn't proved himself at senior level. The centuries he made at the Conservative Club didn't count and perhaps his swagger went against him as well.

Knowles's younger brother said he was 'a big-headed bugger'.

Knowles threatened to sue the governing body if they rejected him a third time and once he was granted his professional status, he started to climb the rankings.

Knowles's profile rose in the first round of the 1982 World Championship.

Unlike others on the circuit, Knowles had no fear of Steve Davis, having beaten him several times when they were juniors.

Davis went into the World Championship as the defending champion and favourite, but that didn't bother Knowles or his manager.

Geoff Lomas made a point of saying within Davis's earshot moments before the players made their entry: 'This fella's got no bottle. Win the first two frames and he'll go under the table.'

Davis was edgy, having a photographer removed early in the match, and Knowles, who was a 150-1 bet for the championship at the start, made few mistakes and grew in confidence.

Davis remembered Knowles escaping a snooker with a swerve shot and then 'twirling his cue around his fingers like a cheerleader's baton as if in an exhibition.

'When I saw him doing that, I thought: "I'm bang in trouble here, if he's enjoying it that much."'

Knowles led 8-1 at the end of the first day, needing only two more frames to wrap up a huge upset.

Even at 8-1 down, there were those who fancied Davis could still get to 10 frames before Knowles, given his resilience.

Earlier in the year, he had rallied from 8-3 down to force a deciding 17th frame against Terry Griffiths in the Lada Classic Final.

Davis went back to his hotel room that he had kitted out in arcade games such as Space Invaders – and Knowles went out clubbing.

'I went to the nightclub, Josephine's, and didn't get back until about 4am, before being back on the table early [10.45am],' he said.

'It relaxed me, I didn't get drunk. I was just winding down and it helped me take my mind off things. Would it have been better to go to the hotel room and think about it all? Not for me.'

It didn't do Knowles any harm. He won the next two frames for a famous 10-1 victory.

Davis remembered years later: 'This was one where I let the outside world in to mess with my usual positive thinking.

'I didn't make it hard for him, got bad vibes about the day, sensed the glee in the crowd that they were loving it and ended up playing the part in succumbing. I thought it was what they wanted and I wasn't strong, stroppy, or thick-skinned enough to change things.'

Knowles went on to beat Graham Miles 13-7 in the second round and was 11-6 up against Australian veteran Eddie Charlton in the best-of-25-frames quarter-final before being unsettled by a noisy spectator.

He finally complained after Charlton drew level at 11-11, but his chance had gone and Charlton went on to win 13-11.

Knowles made a breakthrough later that year when winning the Jameson International, his first tournament success.

The story went, Knowles had three lovers in the audience when he lifted the trophy and that victory brought him a lot of attention.

He told the *Daily Mirror* that in the six months after he beat David Taylor in the final, he received more than 4,000 letters from female admirers.

He said: 'At one tournament a super attractive lady who'd seen me on the box phoned every hotel in the area – and there were a lot – until she found me. She told me she'd booked a table for a candlelit dinner in a nice little country restaurant and then sent a car for me.

'I was curious, so I went. It was a smashing evening.'

Knowles said another sent him a rose every day during a tournament, but was less responsive to some groupies.

'Every time you go into a hotel they follow you,' he said. 'But I have nothing to do with them. If you do, you'll never get rid of them.'

He added: 'I don't see myself as a big sex symbol, even if the ladies say how I've switched them on.'

SUNDAY TABLOID the *News of the World* interviewed Knowles before the 1983 World Championship and his revelations led to them describing him as a 'Lancashire hot pot'.

Asked about snooker groupies, Knowles said: 'I'd be an idiot if I didn't notice them, wouldn't I?'

The headlines didn't distract Knowles and he ended up being one pot away from the final.

He led Cliff Thorburn 15-13 in a best-of-31-frames semi-final – and only had to clear the colours off their spots for victory.

The blue put Knowles one point up, but he left the cue ball closer to the middle pocket than he would have liked. Though cueing was more difficult than it ought to have been, it was a shot Knowles would fancy he would pull off nine times out of ten.

This time, the pink wobbled in the jaws of the pocket and stayed out.

Thorburn rolled in the pink and black for 15-13, but Knowles had another match-winning chance in the next frame. He suffered a horrible miscue when trying a deep screw shot on the final red and Thorburn closed the gap to a single frame.

Thorburn forced a decider that Knowles had a chance to win.

The last red was left hanging on the lip of the green pocket and somehow, Knowles failed to pot it.

Thorburn fluked the red and won the match, leaving Knowles in tears.

THE STORIES ahead of the 1984 World Championship were all about Tony Knowles.

Not many were about how he could go to the top of the world rankings.

If Knowles got further than Davis at the Crucible, he would replace him as world No. 1, but most of the stories written about him around this time made little reference to his snooker ability.

The front page of lads' mag *Titbits* read: 'Why Tony Knowles Can't Say No To Girls' and in the story inside he revealed: 'Women write with the most amazing suggestions and occasionally I take them up on it because I am so curious to find out what they want and it isn't to talk about snooker.'

Knowles was managed by Geoff Lomas at the time and his soon-to-be-ex-wife Helen gave an explosive interview to the *News of the World* on the eve of the World Championship.

She told them: 'It's heartbreaking to see what snooker and success has done to a lot of them. I've seen them come along as nice, open, honest, friendly kids and within a couple of years they're completely ruined. They're totally selfish, wrapped up in themselves and don't care about anyone else. People like Jimmy White, Tony Knowles and Kirk Stevens need full-time nursemaids. They're incapable of looking after themselves.

'They get hold of photos of girls and they use them so they can get them mounted on what they call the Doggie Board, back at one of their houses to keep tally on who is the leading stud.

'Some nights for a laugh they'll see who can pull the ugliest girl and she'll be nominated "Dog of the Week".

'They don't have to try very hard because the girls seem to go on heat the moment they see a snooker player.

'Tony Knowles is the most successful. We call him "The Melter" because the girls just melt when they see him. He can have any girl he wants. They're like putty in his hands.'

There were more revelations in *The Sun*.

'Why Girls Call Me The Hottest Pot In Snooker' was the headline that announced a three-part serialisation of Knowles's private life.

Knowles told the newspaper: 'I never buy them a drink. I never buy them a meal. I never dance with them. The only thing I offer them – apart from myself – is a lift home.'

The interview is best remembered for Knowles saying: 'I don't rate girls out of 10, but out of two – those who say "yes" and those who say "no". I don't meet many who say "no".'

At the Crucible, female officials were seen backstage wearing badges that read 'I Said No To Tony Knowles'.

The backlash continued on the front page of the tabloids after Knowles was beaten 10-7 by John Parrott in the first round.

Ex-girlfriend Julie Saxon talked to *The Sun* for a story that was headed: 'You're A Lousy Lover, Tony'.

Knowles's partner at the time defended her man in a rival tabloid, but the press had turned against him.

Mandy Fisher, the women's world champion, revealed she had managed to say 'no' to Knowles when he made a pass at her.

The *News of the World* decided to follow Knowles when he went to a nightclub during the championship and though he attracted plenty of female attention, there was no story this time.

Knowles was paid £25,000 for the stories he sold to the tabloids, but it cost him more than that.

The World Professional Billiards and Snooker Association fined him £5,000 for bringing the game into disrepute and Barry Hearn estimated the interviews cost him hundreds of thousands of pounds in lost sponsorship.

He described the interviews as 'professional suicide' and *Snooker Scene* wrote of Knowles that his 'apparent willingness to believe his own publicity had obscured his basic good nature, set neutral opinion against him and heaped extra pressure on his shoulders'.

Knowles admitted his mistake years later when, looking back on his career, he said: 'I felt my game deteriorated from that point.'

He remained popular with women. At a tournament in Pontin's, snooker journalist Bill Parsons was handed the job of keeping women away from Knowles so he could concentrate on snooker.

It proved to be an impossible job.

Knowles was docked a frame for turning up late for a semi-final against Willie Thorne that got underway in the morning.

He did win the Australian Masters and then spent the post-match press conference arranging a date with a female reporter before making an early exit from the New Zealand Masters.

He was walloped 3-0 by Jimmy White in only 29 minutes.

Knowles reportedly made a swift exit from a tournament in the United States for another reason. He was wanted by the hot-headed pool champion Earl 'The Pearl' Strickland after a one-night liaison with his long-term girlfriend.

'The fact that Strickland owned a pick-up truck with a fully stocked gun rack behind the driver's seat may have had something to do with it [Knowles's disappearance],' wrote someone on the *Snooker Scene* blog years later.

Knowles went into the 1985 World Championship as the No. 2 seed – despite a meltdown at the Dulux British Open.

Unhappy with Tony Meo's pedestrian pace, Knowles walked off in protest for a few minutes during the third frame, explaining: 'The game was taking so long that I decided that if Tony could take a rest so could I.'

There were those who felt Knowles should have been docked that frame, but he returned to win it to trim Meo's lead to 2-1.

Meo went on to win 5-2 and was blunt about Knowles afterwards. 'He could never live with me as an amateur,' he said, 'but he's had a couple of good results since turning professional and it seems to have gone to his head.

'He's a changed bloke these days and I don't understand him.'

Harvey Lisberg, his former manager, tried to make sense of what was happening to Knowles.

He said: 'His head needs completely curing of a lot of things he's got in it.

'He needs to get over a lot of nonsense he either believes or keeps trotting out. For instance, the excuses every time he gets beat. There's never a reason other than the other bloke's better than you.

'But if you surround yourself with certain types of people, they're going to feed your ego and you're going to end up believing you're better than you really are.'

Perhaps, but Knowles really could play. There was proof his 'A' game made him a match for anyone and when he couldn't find it, he struggled to hide his frustration.

Knowles played some of the best snooker of his career in the first round of the World Championship to turn an 8-5 deficit against Tony Jones into a 10-8 win.

Knowles remembered his quarter-final win over Jimmy White as one of the highlights of his career and he won the opening two frames of his semi-final against Dennis Taylor as well before dramatically falling apart and crashing out 16-5.

Taylor noticed Knowles's fury as the match ran away from him.

Everyone remembers what happened next.

Taylor, who was making his 13th attempt to win the World Championship, faced Steve Davis in the final.

Davis had won eight of their previous nine matches in tournaments and Taylor admitted, 'Every time I played Steve, I tried to block it out.

'I tried not to look at Steve when he was potting. I looked at my shoes or under the table.'

So, he spent most of the opening eight frames of the 1985 World Championship Final looking at his shoes or under the table.

After the first frame of the evening session, it was 8-0 and in the ninth, Davis stretched across the table and stabbed the green towards its pocket. But it didn't drop and Taylor mopped up to register his first frame.

That lifted Taylor and incredibly, at the end of the evening session, the score read Davis 9, Taylor 7.

The match went to a deciding 35th frame, John Williams remembering: 'They were going more grey by the minute and I think they would rather have been anywhere than there for that final frame.'

The spectacle was rather more enjoyable for the 18.5 million viewers who stayed up beyond their bedtime to watch it.

Unless they were waiting for *Bleak House* to start, that is.

That drama was replaced by another that went all the way to the final black.

Davis broke and left the cue ball glued to the top cushion. Taylor fouled and more mistakes followed. 'The balls were awkward,' explained Davis, 'and the pressure made it worse. It was a frustrating frame. There were no clear-cut decisions.' They swapped fouls and although Davis appeared to have the upper hand in the safety exchanges, Taylor put together the first meaningful break, a run of 22 that opened up a 29-13 lead. The break ended when he ran out of position and everyone waited for the decisive moment.

Ted Lowe said: 'The BBC producer, Nick Hunter, came on after midnight and said: "You won't believe this but there's 18.5 million listening to you at the moment." I was in the middle of commentating so I couldn't say "Wow".'

Davis said years later: 'They had to go to work the next morning, but they couldn't turn their televisions off.'

The battle of nerve and wits went on. Taylor fouled again and a neat plant from Davis started what looked like it could be a match-winning break.

But he made a misjudgement when potting the final red and was unable to add a colour, so the break ended at 25 with Davis ahead 53-44.

Still, he laid a snooker that Taylor couldn't escape from and after adding the yellow and fluking the green, Davis was well in control at 18 points ahead with just 22 available. Taylor had to pot all four remaining balls, Davis just one.

Davis missed the brown – so did Taylor. A bad safety shot gave Taylor another chance. The cue ball was near the black spot and the brown hung near the yellow pocket, too close to the side cushion and too far away for it to be a comfortable pot. Taylor remembers thinking: 'I'm going to have a go. I'm not going to lose it playing a safety shot that went wrong.' So he went for the brown – and smacked it in, stunning the cue ball towards the baulk cushion and into position to punch both the blue and pink into the green pocket.

That left him 59-62 behind with just the black left.

The black was on the side cushion. Taylor kissed the trophy – 'I'm going to win you or lose you now,' he said later – and decided to go for the double. 'I couldn't see,' said Davis. 'Dennis was in the way.'

When he heard the crowd's noise rise, Davis must have thought the title was lost, but the black hit the jaw of the middle pocket and ran to safety.

Taylor missed another double and then got the best chance yet. 'I remember thinking: "Just keep your head still, push the cue in and out in a straight line and you will win the world title."'

It didn't happen. 'I had the biggest twitch in the history of the Crucible, I lifted my head in the air, jerked the cue and missed the black by so much that I almost fluked it into the corner I was leaning over. I went back to my seat and thought: "There's no way Steve will miss that black." Everyone was certain Steve would cut the black ball in.'

'I just had to keep it together,' said Davis, who was left sizing up a cut into the bottom left-hand corner pocket. The cue ball was tight on the side cushion and it was a blind pot, meaning he couldn't see the pocket he was aiming at. 'I had to go for it,' said Davis. 'It wasn't easy, but it wasn't difficult. I didn't want to hit it thick and leave it over the pocket.'

So he hit it thin and left it over the pocket. As the crowd roared, the cue ball came off four cushions and rested around the pink spot, leaving Taylor with a simple pot.

'It's a good job the black was over the pocket,' said Taylor after playing the 111th and decisive shot of a frame that ended a nail-biting 68 minutes after it started.

'Can you believe it?' David Vine asked a shell-shocked Davis. 'It's there,' he answered solemnly, 'in black and white.' Later, Davis explained it was a joke and given the circumstances, a pretty good one.

'We played 17 days for one ball and I missed it,' said Davis. 'That's snooker.'

The *Sunday People* would cast doubt over the greatest of all snooker matches four months later with a front-page headline that screamed: 'TV Snooker Sensation: Big Final Was Bent, Says Ex-Manager'.

The ex-manager was Geoff Lomas, who had once had White and Higgins on his books.

The suggestion was the Davis–Taylor final was fixed, but the story didn't reveal anything concrete. Lomas wouldn't name the match he claimed was fixed or provide any evidence and the newspaper was forced to issue an apology.

'TONY KNOWLES Dressed Up In A Girls' Undies', read the front-page headline of *The Sun*.

The claim was made by his ex-fiancée Suzy Harrison. She told the newspaper she broke off the engagement after catching Knowles canoodling with another woman and that led to a furious row during which she was knocked unconscious.

This led to Knowles calling a press conference before the start of the Goya Matchroom Trophy in Stoke-on-Trent.

Knowles denied he had 'at any time sought sexual pleasure through wearing women's underwear or lingerie', but did admit he 'once attended a fancy-dress party with my ex-girlfriend, the outfit for which incorporated some of these items.

'This party was a one-off and I have not attended anything similar since. The party was not in any way perverted or kinky.'

Privately, Knowles was devastated, saying: 'I'd kept a low profile for the previous 18 months.'

This episode was another reminder to the tabloid press that Knowles made good copy.

He was spotted in a nightclub on the morning of the Benson & Hedges semi-final, a match that ended in a 6-4 defeat against Cliff Thorburn.

Manager Howard Kruger told the press: 'He's the sort of person who, if I say: "I want you in bed at 10 o'clock," he won't sleep. He'll watch the video till four in the morning. So I take him out for dinner. What can I tell you? You can't change him overnight.'

Kruger told Knowles to slow down after he was taken to hospital with abscesses and sores all over his body.

There were rumours Knowles was seriously ill, but all he needed was a break from years of hard living and a break from the press.

Knowles told the *Daily Mirror* ahead of the 1986 World Championship: 'It's been absolute bloody hell. I honestly thought I was going crackers ... having a nervous breakdown.'

He played what he described as 'the worst snooker of my life' during his second-round match against Silvino Francisco before pulling through to win 13-10.

That result helped Knowles through to the semi-finals at the Crucible for a third time where he met Bradford's Joe Johnson.

Johnson, without a win in two previous trips to the Crucible, had been ranked a 150-1 outsider by bookmakers at the start of the World Championship and authors Luke Riches and Paul Gadsby described the semi-final clash as being between 'the underachieving Jack The Lad and the overachieving family man'.

It was the 'overachieving family man' who came out on top, Knowles suffering a third semi-final loss by a 16-8 scoreline.

JOE JOHNSON proved to be a popular world champion.

He had a colourful career history – including a spell as a singer in a local band – and every interview he gave indicated he was in no hurry to forget his journey.

Snooker made other headlines that were less heart-warming.

Bookmakers Coral withdrew their sponsorship of the UK Championship and the *Daily Telegraph* wrote as a reaction to the news: 'Infidelity, wife desertion, murmurs of arranged matches and hints of betting coups have brought further discredit. The get-rich-quick attitudes of the governing body, bad management and players' back-street behaviour is killing the game.'

Coral's decision proved to be well timed. The 1986 UK Championship is remembered for Alex Higgins assaulting tournament director Paul Hatherell and Knowles also featured in a bust-up.

Terry Griffiths, the Welshman who was crowned world champion in 1979, said pockets on tables 'have to be on the generous side to make the game attractive ... tighter pockets would suit my game down to the ground. I think I can out-safety play just about everyone in snooker.'

Knowles disagreed, saying: 'When the pockets are too generous, there is no safety play, no subtlety ... What does he know about snooker? He's from the hills and has no idea.

'Terry is usually complaining that the pockets are too small – probably because he can't play the game.'

Higgins supported Knowles, who beat Griffiths 9-6 before bowing out in the quarter-finals, losing 9-4 to John Parrott.

MOMENTS BEFORE Knowles and Neal Foulds started their semi-final in the 1987 Dulux British Open, a woman's garter landed on the table.

This was likely to be a message to Knowles rather than Foulds and it appeared more of a distraction to Knowles.

He lost the opening seven frames in the best-of-17 match and reappeared for the evening session in a new outfit.

The explanation given was that Knowles had mislaid his trousers and had to wear a brown lounge suit instead.

He knew a black bow tie would not go well with the suit and chose not to wear it.

There was another possible explanation. The rumour in the press box was, Knowles had enjoyed a passionate liaison during the break and had discarded his bow tie and raised his shirt collar to hide a love bite.

Whatever had happened, Knowles still went out of the tournament, beaten 9-2.

The management team behind Knowles decided that in a bid to repair the damage done to their player's reputation, they would invite the *Daily Mirror* to his house for an in-depth feature.

It backfired. The headline above Noreen Taylor's piece read: 'Hey, Why Don't We Go To Bed?' and the opening paragraph was a vicious put-down.

'Since that snooker stud label has made him look such a buffoon, it is understandable that Tony Knowles and his advisors are deeply anxious to clean up his tacky, one-night-slag image.'

Asked about tabloid revelations about his private life, Knowles mentioned: 'The bloody bitch who told all them lies about me. If I saw her I'd crack her one on the jaw.'

Knowles' handlers insisted the above was a misquote.

THERE WAS huge interest in Knowles' first-round match at the 1988 Benson & Hedges Masters.

Alex Higgins was returning from a ban that had ruled him out of the five previous tournaments and the Wembley Conference Centre was packed with 2,600 spectators for his match against Knowles, with millions more tuning in to watch on BBC's *Sportsnight*.

There had been friction between the players on Higgins's stag party.

They had to be pulled apart after Higgins accused Knowles of 'pulling my bird', but they went into their match at the Masters on good terms. Higgins thanked

Knowles for talking him through his ban and convincing him to carry on playing snooker.

But there was trouble during the third frame.

At 2-0 down, Higgins accused Knowles of standing in his line of sight.

He went on to snatch that third frame, but Knowles won the next for a 3-1 lead at the interval.

Higgins made a complaint to the tournament director.

Knowles confronted Higgins and countered his claims by accusing him of being so quick to the table he didn't have time to find his seat.

Knowles agreed to sit down as soon as he had finished at the table and the unrest appeared to bother him more than it bothered Higgins. From 3-1 down, Higgins won 5-4, sealing victory with a break of 75.

Knowles was booed by spectators at the post-match autograph session and said: 'He always pulls something like that when he's losing. I was going really well at one stage and fancied it.

'I should have taken him straight out of the arena and put a stop to it, but it all happened so quickly I was caught off guard.'

Higgins sent Knowles two bottles of champagne as an apology (and an admission of guilt). Knowles didn't touch a drop of either.

There was a match during the Masters that became the subject of a police investigation.

The *Daily Mirror* published a story about a betting coup that centred on a match between Terry Griffiths and Silvino Francisco.

Griffiths was a 5-3 winner and after looking into betting patterns and watching videos of the match, the police investigated.

Francisco was arrested, but later released and the case against him collapsed because of a lack of evidence.

ASKED HIS ambition ahead of the 1988 World Championship, Knowles answered it was 'to make love to [tabloid pin-up] Samantha Fox'.

He corrected himself to say his dream was to beat Steve Davis 18-0 in the final and was told by a member of the press: 'Forget it Tony, you have more chance of making love to Samantha Fox.'

His hopes of whitewashing Davis in the final were ended by a quarter-final defeat against Jimmy White and it was a more mature Knowles who was interviewed later that year. He said: 'Perhaps I had life too easy. Perhaps I was too content with what I had. Perhaps I wasn't hungry enough to be a winner again. Sure the press gave me a bad time, but some of it was my fault.'

Knowles proved he could be his own worst enemy ahead of his quarter-final against Davis in the Benson & Hedges Masters. Adrenaline pumping, he said: 'I can't wait to get at the ginger bag of bones.'

Davis whitewashed him 5-0, with Knowles smashing a glass in his changing room during an interval.

Davis said: 'That was his biggest break of the day.'

Knowles promised his revenge at the Irish Masters after labelling Davis 'The Gingerbread Man'.

He said: 'As a kid I used to start by eating the gingerbread man's legs and then the arms until only the smiling face was left. Then you bit the head off. That's what I'm going to do to Steve.'

The boasts backfired spectacularly as Knowles didn't even play Davis after losing to Mike Hallett in the first round.

There were reasons behind Knowles's poor form. It was revealed his relationship with manager Howard Kruger had cost him around £200,000.

Knowles had his eight-year spell in the top 16 of the world rankings ended by a 13-6 defeat against Terry Griffiths in the second round in 1990.

THE CLASS OF '92 AND THE LAUGHING LATVIAN

IF YOU'RE a football fan, the 'Class of '92' means Manchester United legends David Beckham, Ryan Giggs, Nicky Butt, Paul Scholes and brothers Phil and Gary Neville.

They helped United win the FA Youth Cup in 1992 and seven years later they were part of the team that won the trophy treble of the Premier League, FA Cup and Champions League.

To snooker fans, it means something else.

1992 was the year when Ronnie O'Sullivan, John Higgins and Mark Williams joined the professional snooker ranks – and expectations were high.

The World Masters introduced casual snooker fans to the sport's next generation.

Barry Hearn envisaged the World Masters being snooker's equivalent to a Grand Slam tennis event with men's singles and doubles, women's singles and doubles, mixed doubles, a junior tournament – and big prize money.

The prize fund was a record £1 million, with £200,000 going to the winner of the men's singles event, and because the event wasn't sanctioned by the WPBSA, Hearn invited Alex Higgins to take part.

Higgins was banned at the time and upon hearing he had been handed a wildcard, Stephen Hendry, the world champion, threatened to withdraw, a statement that found its way on to the back pages of the *Daily Mail*.

Higgins voluntarily withdrew and, in his absence, White won the men's singles event, beating Tony Drago in the final at the NEC in Birmingham in January 1991.

The junior event was for players aged 16 and under and in his first match, O'Sullivan made a break of 106.

But his interest was ended by John Higgins in the semi-finals and the Scot then walloped Welsh left-hander Mark Williams 6-1 in the final.

During breaks in the final, Higgins's parents, John Sr and Josephine, were interviewed.

They told viewers that after school every day, John Jr would catch a bus to the Masters Club in Denistoun where he was given free time on the table and practised with top pro Alan McManus.

The sessions with McManus had accelerated his progress and though only 15 years old, Higgins was already Scottish under-18 champion as well as under-16 champion.

RONNIE O'SULLIVAN became the youngest snooker rebel when he was thrown out of a tournament – aged only ten years old!

He was playing at the Junior Home Internationals in Prestatyn when he became involved in an altercation with an older boy who he said was nicknamed 'Flash Eddie'.

O'Sullivan was being chased and in an attempt to stop his rival catching up with him, he smashed a glass on the floor.

Referee John Williams ordered O'Sullivan off the site and he was banned from all Pontin's events for a year.

The punishment was slashed to six months.

The story made the pages of *The Sun* newspaper, Britain's most well-read tabloid.

Phil Yates, who went on to be a leading commentator and writer, played O'Sullivan around the same time, at the On Cue Snooker Club in Old Hill in the West Midlands.

O'Sullivan went to the club while visiting his grandparents and was matched with Yates, a capable amateur player.

'I had heard of Ronnie through *Snooker Scene*,' said Yates.

'He made 50 in the first frame.

'I had never seen anything like it. He was so small he couldn't even reach to put the blue back on its spot. It was incredible how good he was.

'He knew where the balls were going to go. He had an extraordinary snooker brain.

'Nobody at that age is guaranteed to become world champion, but Ronnie is the closest I've seen to being that. Even at that age, his talent was extraordinary.'

He also had the backing of his father ...

The O'Sullivans were a colourful family.

Ronnie's paternal grandfather, Micky, had been a professional boxer and his brother Danny was good enough to win the British bantamweight title in 1949.

Dickie completed the trio of fighting siblings, known as 'The Fighting O'Sullivans'.

Ronnie O'Sullivan Sr – known as 'Big Ronnie' – made a fortune out of sex shops.

One way of making money, he discovered, was to post out blank cassettes.

He guessed those receiving them would be too embarrassed to post them back to the company's address.

'Big Ronnie' also instilled in his son the disciplines that would make him a great.

He had to take every practice session seriously and Ronnie Sr wouldn't allow his son to over-celebrate tournament victories. The focus was always on the next tournament.

Ronnie Sr once swapped a car for a snooker cue – and there was no way he was going to let Alex Higgins get his hands on it.

O'Sullivan first met Higgins when he was ten years old at an exhibition at Barking Snooker Club and remembered: 'My dad said: "Don't let him go near your cue."

'It was a collector's item.

'My dad gave away a car for this cue. He said: "Don't let him go near it, he loves cues and will love yours."

'There's a photo of me holding my cue thinking to myself, "Don't let go of it," and Alex looking at it thinking: "That's a nice cue."'

O'Sullivan made his television debut when he was 14 years old.

In 1990, ITV screened the Thames Snooker Classic and viewers saw him make a break of 75 against Steve Ventham before bowing out in the semi-finals.

Hardcore fans were already aware of O'Sullivan's promise.

The previous year he had won the British under-16 title and went on to win a pro-am in Stevenage, beating world No. 34 Marcel Gauvreau on the way to lifting the trophy.

Gauvreau said afterwards: 'No one's ever played that well against me.'

He described O'Sullivan as 'unbelievable'.

ALEX HIGGINS was in no mood to let the 'Class of '92' or anyone else take over snooker.

There was an exchange with Stephen Hendry after the 22-year-old put him out of the 1991 UK Championship.

Higgins says that as he shook Hendry's hand at the end of the match he said: 'Well done Stephen, you were a little bit lucky.'

Hendry told a different story. Higgins, he recalled, said: 'Up your arse, you @@@@.'

Higgins was able to qualify for the Crucible one last time in 1994 after staging an astonishing comeback against Tony Knowles in the final qualifying match.

Trailing 6-3 after the first session, Higgins headed to a nearby pub during the interval.

On his way there, he tripped over a low wall, leaving his arm badly grazed and bleeding.

That didn't stop him sinking several pints and then returning to edge out Knowles in the 19th and deciding frame, leaving spots of blood on the table from his wound.

Higgins knew he was no longer the player he had been and, as his form deteriorated, so did his behaviour.

Daily Star snooker correspondent Dave Armitage watched his decline. 'Alex developed a real problem with the governing body, the WPBSA,' said Dave. 'The less money he earned, the worse his behaviour got. He felt the WPBSA officials were living off the players.

'I remember him walking into a hotel bar late at night and starting to rant and rave. "I hope you're enjoying your drinks, I'm paying for them, you're just a bunch of freeloaders." The next thing, I heard a tremendous clatter.

He had thrown a sizeable glass ashtray at us and it didn't miss by much.

'Alex was led away. He was getting horrible, not just mischievous, and I remember thinking that one day he would go too far.'

Higgins went too far in Dubai. Armitage was leaving a nightclub and Higgins approached him. 'Alex poked me in the face and perhaps unwisely, I punched him,' said Dave. 'He fell down a few stairs, there was a bit of a struggle and I walked away.'

Higgins struggled to walk away from the Crucible after his 10-6 defeat to Ken Doherty in the first round of the 1994 World Championship.

There had been controversy, with Higgins claiming the referee had been standing in his line of sight when he was playing, but Doherty held it together to beat a player who had inspired him to play snooker.

After the match, Higgins stayed in his seat while the arena emptied around him with only his vodka for company.

He was finally convinced to leave and headed to the press conference where he ranted against snooker's governing body and vowed to never play again.

He told the press: 'I ain't playing no more.'

Predictably, Higgins tried to qualify for the 1995 World Championship – and caused trouble.

He had an altercation with referee John Williams when playing Tai Pichit, a former Buddhist monk from Thailand, in Blackpool.

He put together a break that reached 110 when he asked Williams to move.

Williams, regarded as snooker's best referee by O'Sullivan and Joe Davis, said: 'Alex told me

I was standing in his sight line, but I was standing behind him.

'I said: "I'm staying where I am." At that, he burst into tears. He was on the yellow and I remember him turning to me and saying: "You're in my thinking line, if you know what I mean?"

'I said: "I know exactly what you mean, now get on with it."

'He carried on crying and by the end of the break, the tears were pouring down his face.

'Tai went on to win the match and said he didn't want to play Alex again. Maybe Alex should have gone to a monastery and left the world to the rest of us.'

Had he, Williams's job would have been much more straightforward.

'Alex was very complex,' he said. 'I first met him shortly after he had won the World Championship in 1972 and he was fine. I think the press have a lot to answer for. They changed him. They made him out to be a god, a genius and said if it wasn't for Alex, the game would be dead. Alex believed them.

'Alex did play some wonderful shots. He seemed to be making it up as he went along and maybe he was a genius.

'All Alex wanted to do was win and I'm not sure he cared how he won.

'When he started to lose, he could not accept it. Put him in a position where he was likely to lose and he would cause trouble if he could. He liked causing trouble.

'I think he wanted to intimidate the referee into letting something go that they shouldn't or put off his opponent. I tried to ignore him, but it was hard not to take notice of him and if you were nice to him, he took it as a sign of weakness.'

Higgins could be weak himself, as Noel Gallagher recalled.

Gallagher, singer/songwriter of Mancunian scruffs-turned-global-superstars Oasis, recalled: 'Alex Higgins used to live in Burnage [in Manchester].

'He had this house that had triangular windows in, I'm not sure whether he bought the house because it had triangular windows or if he put them in.

'We used to go to his house singing Christmas carols because he was always pissed and he'd always give you money.'

The sleeve of the band's 1995 release 'Roll With It' – their first No. 1 single – featured a photograph of Higgins, who by then was friends with the band.

Liam Gallagher, the band's singer and Noel's younger sibling, said: 'All that money and fame and shit and he's blown the lot. What a fucking way to go. I hope that happens to me. One big fucking blow-out.'

HIGGINS FOUND himself in court in June 1996. He was conditionally discharged after he admitted assaulting a 14-year-old boy after he interrupted a family discussion.

The court heard that 46-year-old Higgins kicked the teenager, a friend of his son Jordan, after he interrupted a discussion between Higgins and his ex-wife Lynn at her house in Greater Manchester.

Defending Higgins, Robin Falvey told the court the defendant described the boy as 'truculent and impertinent' and 'having told him to get out he kicked out with his leg as anybody would'.

Falvey said Higgins was under pressure because of an unspecified illness, and because his ability to earn from the game of snooker was 'virtually negligible'.

Perhaps the Laughing Latvian was going to be the new 'People's Champion'.

STEFAN MAZROCIS would bump into Higgins when both were chiselling out a living in the lower reaches of the rankings, scrapping away for priceless ranking points in front of a handful of snooker obsessives.

'Alex was always very respectful when I saw him at the qualifiers,' remembered Mazrocis. 'He knew how hard it was for us to make a living from playing snooker. Anyway, he was too busy rowing with officials to start rows with the players.'

Mazrocis qualified for the 1995 World Championship and was drawn against the defending champion, Stephen Hendry.

Preparations had gone well.

'I practised with Willie Thorne the day before and knocked in five or six century breaks,' said Mazrocis. 'I was thinking I had a chance against Hendry if I could keep him under pressure. But I just completely froze. I had a chance of winning several of the early frames, but couldn't take them and pretty soon, I was thinking: "I just want to get out of here."

'Before the match, I told myself that whatever happened, I didn't want to end up looking like an idiot and I was starting to look an idiot. I thought I was going to get whitewashed.'

At 5-0 down, that was a possibility, but Mazrocis says his supporters helped him avoid that embarrassment. 'I knew a few of them had money on me winning three frames and they were coughing when Stephen was playing his shots to put him off,' remembered Stefan. He was beaten 10-3 and said: 'I was really disappointed. I didn't play anything like as well as I could. I really didn't enjoy the drive home afterwards.'

Mazrocis qualified again in 1997 and was drawn against Peter Ebdon, a player he knew well.

Ebdon had previously beaten Mazrocis in the World Championship qualifiers and they went further back to the days when both were amateurs.

Ebdon won the World Amateur Under-21 Championship in 1990, Mazrocis was European Amateur Champion in 1989 – and Stefan said: 'Even then, Peter never let his guard down. I knew him for years, but never really knew him.'

Growing up in Islington, Ebdon went to a school around half a mile from Arsenal Football Club's Highbury home and unlike most of his classmates, he supported arch-rivals Tottenham Hotspur instead.

He played the oboe because 'it wasn't the normal instrument that everybody played', but after being given a snooker cue as a present when he was 14 years old, Ebdon discovered that was where his talent lay.

Ebdon was always noticed before he even played a shot.

The others dressed in T-shirt and jeans – but Ebdon always wore a suit.

He made a huge impact on his World Championship debut after turning pro.

The pony-tailed newcomer told his local newspaper ahead of the 1992 event that he 'fully expected' to be crowned champion and he ousted No. 3 seed Steve Davis by a 10-4 scoreline in the first round.

Ebdon bowed out in the quarter-finals to Terry Griffiths. He went into the match with Mazrocis at the 1997 World Championship ranked No. 3 in the world and with a reputation for being a steely, win-at-all-costs competitor.

He played with a furrowed brow intensity and was known as 'Psycho'; Mazrocis played with a pint glass in his hand and was nicknamed the 'Laughing Latvian'.

Stefan's father was Latvian, but he was born and raised in Blaby, a suburb of Leicester where, inspired by watching snooker on television, he used a fire poker to push marbles around the kitchen table at the family home.

His parents invested in a 5ft 2½in table and as a teenager, he was given a key to the local GEC Club and would practise there after school. Stefan made his first century break aged 14 and joined Willie Thorne's club in Leicester city centre where, blinking through a fug of cigarette smoke, he would see Steve Davis, Dennis Taylor and Cliff Thorburn perfecting their potting.

From the age of 16, Mazrocis travelled the country with Thorne playing money matches.

'Willie would back me,' he said. 'He would give me the stake money, then disappear for a few hours and if I had lost, he would win the money back. But I hardly ever lost. We won a lot of money.'

Stefan remembers being edged out 6-5 by Steve James, who went on to be ranked as high as No. 7 in the world, and losing £2,000. But not for long. 'Willie challenged him to a match and offered him an 80-point lead,' said Mazrocis. 'But Willie only had to win one frame and Steve had to win five. Willie won the second frame.

'I was playing some of the best amateurs around, but at the time, Willie was among the best professionals in the world.'

Mazrocis remembers watching Thorne compile 'around 20 century breaks' during an afternoon, counting out thousands of pounds and handing him money to bet on horses and dogs.

Mazrocis practised at Thorne's club in Leicester in the build-up to the 1997 World Championship.

He practised ten hours every day and made three maximum 147s in one afternoon, with teenager Mark Selby on the receiving end twice!

'Mark had just started out and I used to give him a 40-point head start back then,' said Mazrocis.

Mazrocis had beaten Ebdon twice in Holland in the weeks leading up to their match at the Crucible where Mazrocis was backed by what he described as 'the noisiest, worst-behaved crowd in the history of snooker'.

He explained: 'I was scared I might freeze up again. I took a few friends with me who I knew were going to mess about. They weren't going to treat it like a big occasion, just a lads' day out and that's what I wanted. I just went there to have a good time. That was the attitude I had and I knew if I could show Peter I wasn't scared of him, I had a chance.'

Mazrocis lost the opening frame and remembered: 'I sank a great red in the second frame, then cleared up and he knew he was in a game.'

Mazrocis celebrated by sinking the first of many pints. 'I would just catch the eye of one of the officials, point at my glass and they would bring me another pint,' he laughed.

He kept drinking and winning frames. Mazrocis was also getting under Ebdon's skin. He remembers a safety exchange in the opening session when they took it in turns to prod away at the pack of reds – and each other's patience – until Ebdon snapped.

'I didn't bother sitting down in between shots,' said Mazrocis. 'I just hung around near the cameramen waiting for my turn. Peter turned to me and said: "Are you going to sit down?" I knew he was under pressure.'

By his own admission, Mazrocis had 'had a few drinks by then' and snapped back. 'I called him a twat,' he said, 'and that changed the match. It became personal. There was needle there.'

Mazrocis sensed Ebdon may be coming apart mentally – 'I knew I had got under his skin' – and changed his game plan. It was to have no game plan.

He would recklessly plough the cue ball into the pack and back himself to out-pot Ebdon, who was clearly rattled by Stefan's carefree approach. Mazrocis was playing with all the freedom of someone who had earned the chance to play at the World Championship by winning a raffle.

'As soon as we said those words, I just decided I was going to laugh my head off at everything,' laughed the Laughing Latvian. 'I just didn't want to feel any pressure. I was smashing into the reds, he was missing shots and I just sat there laughing.

'I decided to go for absolutely everything and then change it if things went wrong. But the balls kept flying in and he kept missing.'

Mazrocis kept drinking as well.

He sank a crucial pink in the fifth frame that was later named runner-up in BBC Television's Shot of the Championship. Clive Everton, reporting on the match for *Snooker Scene*, wrote that the Midlander's clearance from the brown in that frame 'defied orthodox shot selection mentality'.

He continued: 'Having run out of position on the pink, with the cue ball tight under the top cushion and the black hanging over a corner pocket, the only option for Mazrocis appeared containment. Instead, he audaciously smashed the pink to a baulk pocket.'

'THE HURRICANE' AS A YOUNG MAN ... Alex Higgins at the 1972 World Championship

WHAT DO I DO NOW? Jimmy White weighs up his options while Alex Higgins looks on during the 1982 World Championship

*CIGARETTES AND ALCOHOL
… Alex Higgins at the 1983 World
Championship*

CHALK AND CHEESE . . . Steve Davis sips water, while Alex Higgins lights a cigarette

'COCAINE' KIRK . . . Stevens lived a rock and roll lifestyle

MR MAXIMUM . . . Willie Thorne outside Osborne's Snooker Club in Leicester in 1976

'THE MELTER'... Tony Knowles thinks over a switch to American football

'THE WHIRLWIND'... Jimmy White at the table in 1986

'THE ROCKET'... Ronnie O'Sullivan chills out in 2001

POT WHACK! ... Mark King (left) and Quinten Hann slug it out in the boxing ring

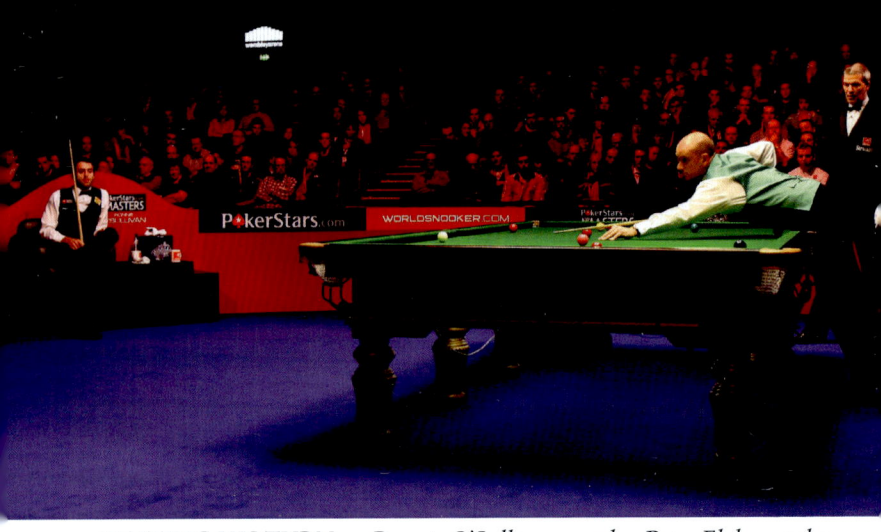

WAITING HIS TURN . . . Ronnie O'Sullivan watches Peter Ebdon at the table in 2010

MAKING A POINT … Ronnie O'Sullivan at the 2023 World Championship

The black made it 4-1, then it became 5-1 and 6-1 to Mazrocis. Ebdon pegged back the eighth frame to trail 6-2 overnight and when the match restarted, nothing had changed.

'Peter was exactly the same,' said Mazrocis. 'He just couldn't shake off whatever was in his head. He couldn't keep his concentration and I was stealing frames. I knew the only way I would lose was if I beat myself.'

That didn't happen. Mazrocis held his nerve – and his pint glass – but it was a miss by Ebdon that denied the Crucible audience and the watching millions what would have been 'one of the greatest-ever snooker moments', according to Stefan.

'I was 7-2 up and he was making a clearance,' said Mazrocis. 'He was knocking down the colours and I just knew that after he sank the final black, he was going to shake his fist and shout something. I decided I was going to jump out of my seat and shout: "Come on, Peter, you can do it!" It would have been hilarious, but he missed the final black, so I never got the chance. It's a shame. I think that would have been one of the greatest-ever snooker moments.'

Mazrocis had to be content with a 10-3 win and what Clive Everton described as 'the biggest Crucible upset of the 90s and arguably since Tony Knowles drubbed Steve Davis 10-1 in 1982'.

'It wasn't a brilliant game,' admitted Mazrocis of a match that produced a highest break of just 77 for the winner, but the post-match interview was better.

'I remember sitting there in front of 20 or 30 reporters talking absolute bollocks!' said Mazrocis. 'I told them I usually drink more than that during a match and had them in stitches for about 20 minutes. My mates said to me afterwards, "What were you going on about?" because I'm not really a drinker, but I was just having fun.

'Peter didn't say a word to me afterwards.'

The following day, 'Lager Clout' was the headline on the back page of *The Sun*, but Ann Yeats, the tournament director, was less impressed. 'She told me it wasn't the image snooker wanted,' said Stefan, 'but I was having fun and I think that appealed to a lot of people.'

Mazrocis wasn't breaking any rules, so he carried on drinking throughout his second-round match with Canadian Alain Robidoux.

At 8-3 down and having lost six successive frames, Mazrocis decided it was time for a rethink. 'I almost fell over,' he said, 'and knew I had to stop drinking and get my game together.'

Mazrocis did trim the deficit to 9-7, but couldn't get in front. 'He always had that lead over me,' said Stefan, 'but I played really well.'

Having laughed and drank his way on to the back pages, Mazrocis looked like he could be the next People's Champion – a caption in *Snooker Scene* described him as 'the hope of the drinking classes' – and it looked like there was a vacancy.

Jimmy White's 10-9 defeat to Anthony Hamilton in the first round ended his 15-season unbroken spell in the top 16 of the world rankings and Higgins was struggling.

But Mazrocis never appeared at the Crucible again. He won money betting on Ebdon when he won the World Championship in 2002 before a tragedy brought them back to face each other again.

Stefan decided to arrange a charity match after a friend from Milton Keynes died in a car crash. 'The club was absolutely packed,' said Mazrocis, 'and it was definitely a grudge match. We said hello before the game and I thanked him for coming, but that was about it. We were never going to be friends.'

Mazrocis broke off in the opening frame, leaving Ebdon a long red that he fired in. 'It was the best shot I've ever seen,' said Mazrocis, 'and he went on to make a maximum.'

The first four frames were shared and Ebdon went on to win the match 5-3.

'Peter is a class player and showed it,' said Mazrocis.

By then, Mazrocis was making a living playing on the European circuit. He was based in Holland and played in tournaments in Germany, Austria and Belgium.

He returned to the Main Tour for the 2008/09 season, but said, 'I hardly won a match,' and decided to concentrate on private coaching, mainly in Germany and Belgium.

ONE NIGHT WITH THE HURRICANE

ALEX HIGGINS turned up in Plymouth in August 1997 as the 155th-best snooker player in the world.

He was hoping to be one of eight players to win a place on the Main Tour and that prize was enough to tempt Neil Mosley out of retirement.

He was ranked 26 places below Higgins at No. 181, but five years earlier, he had sat on top of the snooker world.

Reaching the final of the English Amateur Championship, where he was beaten by Stephen Lee, earned Mosley a trip to the World Amateur Championship in Malta in 1992.

He lifted the trophy and added the European and English titles in the following months, fulfilling the promise he had shown as a teenager growing up in Peterlee, County Durham.

'I started playing on a six-foot table when I was 12,' remembered Mosley, 'and I went on to play at the Miners' Welfare when I was a teenager. I didn't really go to school much after that. I found a way to make money, so school wasn't a top priority.

'My parents split up and mam was getting £36 per week and when I won the *Northern Echo* under-16s I came home with £50.

'I went around winning £50 and £100 from tournaments. My mam thought I was thieving. Mam couldn't believe it. There was one time she was going to ring the police. She thought I must have broken into somewhere. She didn't realise you could make money playing snooker. She thought I had gone to play snooker and then robbed somewhere on the way home!'

The professional circuit proved to be a hard grind, Mosley saying: 'There were only five or six tournaments and 600 players turning up for qualifying events.

'You would have to win nine games to earn £100. I remember playing matches and thinking: "Even if I win, I haven't got the money for a bed and breakfast, I will have to sleep in my car." I slept in the changing rooms once.

'I went from being world amateur champion, and having people paying for me to stay in hotels, to that.'

Mosley found jobs that paid rather better for a while, until he found out about the tournament in Plymouth.

'They put tour cards up for grabs,' he said, 'and someone convinced me to have a go.

'There were four events and if you got far enough you got a tour card.'

Mosley hadn't played competitively for a few months and on his return to action, he was drawn against Higgins.

'I had heard a few stories (about Higgins),' he said, 'but it was the weirdest match and the weirdest few days of my life.

'This was before he got really ill [with cancer]. He looked quite dapper and thought he was making a comeback, but it was evident from the start he was gone.

'He was very poor. I remember him playing some good safety shots, but he let himself down by missing some easy balls.

'He was saying I was standing in the line of his shot, making noises and moving.

'I didn't dare to take a drink of water because every time I moved he said I was trying to put him off.

'I went to the toilet once and he said I kept going to the toilet. I only went once!

'After the game, you had to write down any complaints you had about the referee and he wrote: "He's the devil."

'I heard them rowing and he picked on me, but I'm a big lad so that didn't go very far.

'I went up for a beer with a few of the lads and he came in and he was a completely different person.

'I ended up drinking with him for two days. It nearly killed me. We went to one place where he ended up on stage with his top off, singing. There was trouble with the bouncers and I ended up being his bodyguard.

'We were in a taxi and I said, "I can't drink any more, I need to go to bed," but he still went on somewhere.

'I never knew anyone who won't sleep or eat. He would have a pint of Guinness and a whisky every 15 minutes and thought a meal was a pint of milk. That was his dinner.

'I had to sleep for three days after being with him and I was a young man at the time.'

There was an ugly side to Higgins.

Mosely said he was also 'the rudest man I've ever met. If there were ten people around him he would be the life and soul of the party, telling stories and then he would just zone in on one person he didn't like the look of and try to humiliate them.

'I had a friend with me who went to public school and who talked posh and Alex hated him.

'I had to put my finger on Alex's nose and tell him.

'I remember one night we were sat there drinking and he was telling me how he had lost £200,000 betting on a horse race and that the WPBSA should give him money because of everything he had done for the game.

'I told him straight. I said he was a disgrace. I told him: "You had a beautiful wife and a lovely house and now you have nothing. You're a waste of space." I told him that I had to work behind bars to scrape together the money to enter tournaments and there were hardly any tournaments to enter.

'I woke up the next day and found out he had been hit with an iron bar.'

Higgins was found lying outside a nightclub claiming he had been attacked.

He discharged himself from hospital and headed to the home of Holly Hayse, a girlfriend who was allowing him to live in a caravan in her garden.

They had a row which ended with Hayse stabbing Higgins several times. She was acquitted in court, Higgins declining to give evidence, and said afterwards: 'I still love him deeply. I want to marry him and put his life back on the rails.'

Higgins never did seem set for a happy ending and doctors gave him only eight months to live after diagnosing him with throat cancer in June 1998.

He was still alive 12 months later to tell Irish television: 'I just accepted it. I just went through what I had to go through.'

Higgins took the chance to deny he was ever an alcoholic, explaining: 'I have always been a restless cat. People don't understand that I'm hyperactive.'

He was bitter about his treatment by snooker's governing body, the World Professional Billiards and Snooker Association. 'I haven't had a lot of help from my association,' he said. 'My ears are ringing from the general public telling me it [snooker] wouldn't be anything without me.'

Higgins went on to announce he planned to sue two tobacco companies. The 50-year-old revealed he had undergone 44 doses of radiotherapy and had surgery to remove a cancerous lymph node in his neck, a result of his tobacco addiction.

He had been smoking since he was 15 years old and friends estimated he smoked up to 80 cigarettes a day.

The Dublin solicitor Higgins hired said he wanted around £200,000 for his pain and suffering, along with compensation for around 20 years of lost earnings up to the retirement age of 65.

He said he had 'nothing but disgust' for the tobacco industry when interviewed by the BBC for the *Tobacco Wars* documentary that was screened in July 1999.

'The tobacco companies and snooker were as thick as thieves,' he hissed, his throat ruined by cancer. 'Obviously I think that they have got their advertising for a song for 25 years. Cigarettes are everywhere in snooker. Freebies everywhere. Most players were given free cigarettes.'

THE FOLLOWING summer, Reg Warland was in a Blackpool pub when he saw 'someone at the bar wearing a long coat, looking very scruffy, nursing a pint'.

As he got closer, Warland realised who it was.

Higgins spotted Warland looking at him, his eyes narrowed and he whispered: 'I know you.'

'Of course you do. I was with Willie Thorne, remember all that fun we used to have back in the old days.

'I'm going to the toilet and then I will get us both a drink and something to eat.'

Higgins nodded, but when Warland returned to the bar, he was gone. 'He was embarrassed by the state he was in,' said Warland. 'He knew he looked like a tramp.'

Higgins didn't appear to have long to live, but incredibly, he announced his intention to play snooker competitively again, two years later.

He entered the Benson & Hedges Championship, that was played at the Towers Snooker Club in Mansfield in October 2002. The winner qualified for the Benson & Hedges Masters at Wembley the following February, a tournament Higgins had won twice.

He had paid a £30 deposit to enter and a further £200 to enter the World Championship.

Tickets for his comeback match in Mansfield were priced at £3 and being sold for £100 on the black market.

One friend promised the crowd would be entertained, saying Higgins was making breaks of 70 or 80 and adding: 'He still loves the game. He misses his fans and the crowd.'

Not everyone was looking forward to the spectacle.

John Higgins reckoned 'it's terrible for the game if he's going to be coming back in the state that he's in'.

Alex responded in the tabloids by suggesting 'a little match' between them.

That came to nothing and to the disappointment of those who splashed out to see him in Mansfield, Higgins was forced to pull out, explaining: 'I need to get some dental work done.'

He hoped to be ready for the forthcoming World Championship qualifiers, to be held at the Manhattan Snooker Club in Harrogate.

To qualify for the Crucible, Higgins would have to win around 12 matches and though he paid his £200 entry fee, he decided to pull out again, citing health issues.

Once he was well enough, Higgins went back to hustling around pubs and clubs. Taxi drivers in Belfast remembered how Higgins would walk into a club, find out who had money in their pocket and befriend them.

Higgins would attempt to milk them for drinks and play them at pool or snooker for money before moving on to the next ...

One who knew Higgins at this time said: 'We've all felt sorry for him, bought him beers, given him a few bob, even given him somewhere to get his head down.

'But he always ends up abusing your good deeds and we've all given up on him.'

The Independent newspaper became aware that Higgins had been booked to play an exhibition at a pub in Shepherd's Bush in January 2003, his first public appearance in Britain since the loss to Mosley.

Punters were asked to pay £30 to play Higgins at pool, an offer that attracted what the reporter described as 'the pond life of west London'.

Higgins was 'pale, hollow-cheeked, his body ruined by abuse' and his audience 'gathered around the table to cheer on their anti-hero playing against an assortment of pub regulars – Harry and Eamon and a man resembling Minnesota Fats in girth if not guile. The atmosphere was thick with anticipation and cigarettes'.

Higgins, who was living with one of his sisters having spent time in a homeless hostel, wore 'an ill-fitting shirt and waistcoat' and 'began badly, the cue ball cannoning in-off a yellow, surprising his opponent, who had sat down, not expecting to be back at the table quite so soon.

'As the night wore on, he [Higgins] enlisted sympathetic cheers for missing relatively easy pots' and the night ended with Higgins muttering to himself, 'I just want to go home to bed,' while he signed autographs.

FOR A while, Richard Dormer became Alex Higgins and it almost broke him.

Dormer remembered meeting Higgins in an interview with the *Belfast Telegraph* in 2013.

'He was ordering a pint of Pernod,' Dormer said.

'We shared the journey back to Belfast. He wanted to swap jackets with me, but my girlfriend had given it to me as a present and I didn't want to. He told me where to go.

'It was a bad start. But at the end of the journey he came over to me with a bottle of Tennent's and said: "No hard feelings, kid." I just thought: "He's a good guy."'

That meeting inspired Dormer to write the play *The Hurricane*.

It started at a 100-seat-capacity venue in Belfast and moved on to the Edinburgh Fringe Festival where Dormer was awarded the Best Actor award.

The Hurricane also won the BBC Stewart Parker Award for New Writing and toured the country.

Dormer said: 'I got so under the skin of the man that I felt I was looking out at the world through his eyes. I developed a restless energy, little nervous tics, the weight dropped off me, I couldn't eat properly, I developed insomnia, I became quick to anger and intolerant of ignorance and rudeness in people, my moods fluctuated constantly, I started thinking at a lightning speed, seeing hidden slights in conversations and paranoid at every meeting that someone was trying to exploit my talent. I started to think I was turning into Alex.

'It was exhausting ... I said so to Alex. He just looked at me with those big blue eyes and said: "How do you think I feel? I've been playing me since before you were born."'

Higgins was in the audience when Dormer performed *The Hurricane* at the London Arts Theatre in 2004. He took his place in the seats and lit a cigarette. The venue was non-smoking and spotting the smoke, an attendant approached Higgins and told him to stub it out. Higgins argued that, given the play was about him, he should be allowed to smoke if he wished to do so. The dispute was resolved when Higgins agreed to finish his cigarette outside.

THE RECEPTIONIST at St Macartans School in Drumaness had an unusual phone call one morning in February 2003.

Margaret Dornan was ringing to say her son Darren wouldn't be at school that day – because he was playing Alex Higgins in the Irish Snooker Championship.

Only 16 years old, Dornan was one of eight amateurs who qualified for the championship and was drawn against Higgins in the first round, over the best of nine frames.

'I was playing in a local league and got a phone call saying: "You're playing Alex Higgins at two o'clock tomorrow,"' he remembered.

'I just thought, "Jesus, this is a once-in-a-lifetime opportunity."

'People were saying the draw had been fixed. There was a lot of hype about Higgins making a comeback and they thought the organisers wanted him to win so they put him in with a 16-year-old.

'If that's the case, it backfired!'

Colin Maguire was promoting the event and he also happened to be Higgins's manager at the time. He told the press before the Dornan match that Higgins could still 'beat anyone on his day'.

That was the hope of the majority of the crowd – all 89 of them.

The venue held 809 spectators, but with the draw only revealed the night before, there was no chance of it being anywhere near full.

Many of the 89 were reporters, much to Higgins's annoyance.

'There must have been ten photographers at the bottom of the table taking photos when we shook hands before the match,' said Dormer.

'Alex was squeezing my hand and saying to me: "These people are poison." He hated the press.'

The start was delayed after the referees were stuck in traffic and the organisers found someone from the crowd to take charge, Kevin Hughes.

Dornan said: 'I broke off and was standing near my seat chalking my cue.

'Alex was down on his shot and then he got up, he walked over to me and said: "When I'm at the table, kid, you stay in your seat."

'I sat down straight away. I was shaking. My dad had told me he had headbutted officials and punched referees. Dad told me: "Don't give him any ammunition."'

Higgins said afterwards: 'The referee they got off the street said to me [before the match], "No fighting and no head butting."'

Nobody told Higgins he couldn't complain and at the end of the opening frame, he accused Hughes of being unable to count and had him replaced.

'I knew after the first frame he wasn't going to make an 80 break,' said Dornan, 'but at the same time I thought:

"He still won two world titles, maybe he can still turn it on?" He did still pot some great balls.'

Higgins won the third frame with a break of 23 and knowing he was sure to lose, he looked for someone to blame. He told a photographer with menace: 'If you do that once more ...' and midway through the fourth frame he went into the crowd looking for a reporter.

He asked: 'Which one's *The Independent*?'

Higgins located the reporter and asked him at the end of the frame: 'I've heard you want to talk to me. How much are you paying?'

Higgins was told there would be no payment and he said: 'I can't afford to talk for nothing these days.'

Dornan held himself together to win 5-1 and one disappointed spectator wrote to *Snooker Scene* to say how poorly Higgins had played – and how he looked for people to bully.

Dornan was thumped 6-1 by Joe Swail in the next round and said: 'I met him [Higgins] a few times afterwards and he said: "I want a rematch."

'I mentioned it to the guy who ran the club where I played. I was saying, "We could get a few people here," and he said, "No chance. We chucked Higgins out of here 40 years ago and we're never having him back."'

Dornan and Higgins ended up playing each other in an exhibition elsewhere.

'I beat him again and he didn't take it too well,' said Dornan.

'Every match he wanted to play for £20. We played ten games and he must have lost eight.

'People were asking him for photos and he wanted a fiver. People were saying: "Stuff your photo." He was down and out.'

'I THINK I was the most natural, charismatic player who ever lifted a cue,' said Higgins when interviewed ahead of the Snooker Legends Tour in February 2010.

'I think my presence around the table was mesmerising at times. It captured people. I'm not telling you this to bolster my ego. It's what people tell me. People stop me in the street every day and say: "When you coming back Alex, when you going to show these so-and-sos who claim to be snooker players how to play the game?" I say I'm not healthy enough as yet. But I'd love to.'

The frail Higgins was convinced that, despite being more than a decade removed from his last significant victory on the tour, he could still prove to be a match for the top 32 in the world.

'The cancer robbed me of my teeth,' he said. 'I would need to have proper teeth, then I could eat properly. I need to gain two and a half stone in weight, get that power back in my arm.

'And I would need to play with fellow professionals I like, people who enjoy playing. But given the right conditions, I could be at least as good as anybody in the top 32.'

Higgins gave proof he still had something left of the skills that took him to the world title twice by putting together a break of 65 in front of the reporter, who wrote: 'He doesn't walk round the table, he dances. On tiptoe, delicate, elegant, he spins off after every shot as if in a waltz with the cue.'

'It all comes from the feet,' explained Higgins. 'Every sport's the same. Snooker's no different. It's all about balance.

'I once made a 118 break in two minutes and four seconds. The reason I was so quick, I was impatient. I couldn't wait to hit the next shot. I could think six shots ahead. It's no different than chess. That was me, I was more or less a chess player.'

For all his bravado, Higgins was living in sheltered housing on Donegal Road in Belfast and when Cliff Thorburn saw him on the opening night of the Snooker Legends Tour, at the Crucible Theatre in April 2010, he burst into tears.

Only a week or so earlier, Higgins had been discharged from hospital after battling pneumonia and he looked close to death.

But Higgins was still Higgins, going for risky shots and looking at his cue accusingly whenever he missed.

He could only manage a highest break of eight in two frames against Thorburn and it was his safety play and judgement of the table's angles that kept him in the opener down to the colours before Thorburn won the second more comfortably.

Later that month, an interview with Higgins appeared in the Sunday tabloid, the *News of the World*. The reporter found him weighing barely six stones (38kg) and surviving on £200 a week benefits and a diet of baby food.

Twelve years earlier, his teeth had fallen out during radiotherapy as he fought cancer and Higgins struggled to find food to eat.

'There are days,' he said, 'I cannot get out of bed. I just lie there and listen to the radio. I'm so weak, I don't have a choice. You can't eat, you can't smile. It causes deep depression.'

Higgins was trying to raise £20,000 for teeth implants that his dentist believed would help him eat properly again. 'You don't know what that will be like, to be able to sit down and have a proper meal again,' he said.

The interview with Higgins was published alongside a report of 52-year-old Steve Davis reaching the quarter-finals of the World Championship with a victory over defending champion John Higgins that was described as 'the greatest Crucible upset ever'.

Davis was then well beaten 13-5 by Neil Robertson, an Australian left-hander.

Robertson went on to reach the final, where he defeated Graeme Dott 18–13.

Higgins watched the match in his cramped Belfast flat 'with only his Guinness, his roll-ups and his anger for company', according to author Simon Hattenstone.

Higgins's supporters did raise the £20,000 needed for teeth implants, but after travelling to Spain, Higgins was told he was too fragile to undergo the operation.

The end was near.

On 24 July 2010, Higgins didn't answer his mobile phone when friends rang and they broke down the door of his sheltered accommodation to find him dead aged 61 and with only £80 left of what had once been an estimated £4 million fortune.

Clive Everton concluded in his obituary of Higgins in *Snooker Scene*: 'Perhaps he would have won more titles if he had lived even a slightly more temperate life, but full throttle, all-out death or glory on and off the table was his style and, for all his faults, snooker is lucky to have had him.'

The Higgins boast had always been that he would have a bigger funeral than footballer George Best, another of Belfast's sporting icons.

Best had died in November 2005 aged 59, after struggling for years with alcoholism.

Thousands lined the funeral route on the day Higgins was laid to rest – including Dean Begley.

He told the BBC: 'I played against Alex in a club in Rosemary Street last year. He was still potting century breaks, I couldn't believe how well he was still playing.'

'THE ROCKET' AND HIS RIVALS

'IF I was left to my own devices, I would be on a beach in Spain putting deckchairs up, having a cup of tea, reading the paper and plodding along ...'

Once he saw his son play snooker, Ronnie O'Sullivan Sr made other plans for him.

'My uncle got a [snooker] table for his son and I went over and started playing,' remembered Ronnie Jr.

'It was good, but I couldn't pot a ball to save my life. They [his parents] got me a table for Christmas and I wasn't allowed to play on it until Christmas. We had it in the house for two weeks and he [Ronnie Sr] kept saying: "You're not playing on it." I used to cry and he used to play all his mates.'

O'Sullivan Sr would say he knew his son had potential when he was 'taking a few quid off me' and decided he would fund his snooker career by paying for practice sessions at a local club.

'I got off on the snooker environment,' said Ronnie. 'It was good banter. The lads were always taking the mickey out of each other and playing pranks. It was a good buzz.'

O'Sullivan studied Steve Davis's technique and started to collect trophies on the junior circuit the way Davis did as a professional in his 1980s prime.

No matter what O'Sullivan did, it wasn't enough for his father.

'Even if I won a tournament, he said: "It's history. It's over. Forget it. Move on,"' said Ronnie Jr.

ITV had their cameras on the O'Sullivans during the 1990 Thames Snooker Classic when 14-year-old Ronnie Jr reached the last four.

'It was all downhill after,' he said a couple of decades and many trophies later. 'It was.'

O'Sullivan would later say he 'was playing a professional game at 13' and he was 16 years old when he joined the paid ranks.

He was the player the sport – and the tabloid press – had been waiting for.

Here was a teenage talent – hailed as 'a genius' by those in the know – who played fast, lived fast and was forever fighting his rivals, authority and most damaging of all, himself.

O'Sullivan faced all his battles without his father.

The day after O'Sullivan became the youngest to qualify for the World Championship, Ronnie Sr was sentenced to life in prison for murder.

The previous October, while his son was playing at a tournament in Amsterdam, 'Big Ronnie' had been at a nightclub on the King's Road in Chelsea and stabbed Bruce Bryan to death with a six-inch hunting knife.

The judge ruled he should serve a minimum of 18 years for an offence that appeared to be racially motivated.

'I thought he was going to come home,' said O'Sullivan years later. 'Everyone was saying it was an accident, really, two people in the wrong place at the wrong time.

'I didn't expect it. It killed me. I didn't know what to do. People were telling me: "He ain't coming home."

'I couldn't get my head around it. I got out of bed the next morning and it was quiet. He ain't quiet, he chats, he's a people person. I was demotivated. I had nobody to tell me what to do.'

Unsurprisingly, O'Sullivan made a first-round exit from the 1993 World Championship, losing 10-7 to Alan McManus, but later that year he won the UK Championship at 17 years, 358 days, making him the youngest player to ever win a ranking event.

O'Sullivan made three century breaks during his 10-6 win over Stephen Hendry in the final that secured a £70,000 cheque and changed his life.

'I went from no one knowing me and the next day I went to have breakfast and people were pointing at me,' he said.

O'Sullivan found himself the centre of attention when he went to visit his father at Gartree Prison in Leicestershire.

'I went to see my dad and TV crews were there and I thought, "What's going on?"' he said.

'I wanted to say [to his father]: "That's for you." That put a lot to rest. I proved: "You ain't to blame. We can move on."

'He patted me on the back and said: "Go and get another one."'

O'Sullivan kept tabloid reporters busy in the coming months.

He reportedly shrugged off smashing up a £36,000 car because he had the money to go out the next day to buy a new one.

There was also the revelation that O'Sullivan was late getting to rehearsals for television show *Big Break* because he was having sex with a contestant in his changing room.

There were more headlines after O'Sullivan's mother, Maria, was convicted of evading VAT payments of £250,000 in July 1995, and sentenced to seven months in prison.

O'Sullivan fell apart.

The loss of both parents and the responsibility of looking after 12-year-old sister Danielle was too much.

'I went mental,' he said. 'I lost the plot. I went out and had a good time. Nobody was there telling me what to do. I was drinking and puffing [cannabis] like mad to make up for my lack of confidence.'

The expectation was that Maria O'Sullivan would be released from prison in January 1996, but she was charged with helping run the family's pornography business, on the instruction of Ronnie Sr, from prison.

There was a reprieve after two jurors admitted they had read an article in *The Sun* newspaper that the judge ruled may prejudice the case.

Maria was freed and faced the challenge of getting her son under control.

It wasn't an easy job.

O'Sullivan ran into trouble during his first-round match at the 1996 World Championship.

He opened up an 8-2 lead over Alain Robidoux and with the 11th frame about to be wrapped up, O'Sullivan switched to play three shots left-handed.

Robidoux took this badly and once O'Sullivan missed, he refused to concede, though his cause was hopeless.

O'Sullivan responded by refusing to pot the pink that would have won him the frame – even when it hung over pocket.

This went on for eight minutes – live on BBC Television.

There was no handshake after O'Sullivan wrapped up a 10-3 win and he said afterwards: 'I didn't give him any respect because he didn't deserve any.'

O'Sullivan later apologised, but got into more trouble after seeing off Tony Drago in the second round.

Michael Ganley, the assistant press officer, told O'Sullivan's friend, Del Hill, to leave the players' room because he was wearing jeans and after he was told, O'Sullivan erupted.

He headbutted Ganley and after O'Sullivan spotted him on the phone to tournament organiser Ann Yates, he grabbed his testicles.

O'Sullivan would later say he was 'ashamed', but still, there was a chance he would be thrown out of the championship.

There was a meeting to decide whether O'Sullivan should be allowed to go ahead with his quarter-final against John Higgins. It was decided that O'Sullivan should be allowed to stay in the championship, but he was handed a two-year suspended sentence and fined £20,000.

He also made voluntary contributions to two charities.

O'Sullivan went on to beat Higgins and lose to Peter Ebdon by a 16-14 scoreline in the semi-finals before finding his private life splashed across the tabloids again.

Sally Magnus announced she was pregnant with O'Sullivan's child. The relationship with O'Sullivan was casual, on his behalf anyway. He told the press Magnus was not his 'bird'.

In the summer of 1996, Maria O'Sullivan decided she'd had enough.

Ronnie had ballooned to 15 stones (95kg) through excessive drinking and eating and Maria asked him to leave the family home.

'I can't stand this no more,' she told him. 'Watching you throw your life away. I'm embarrassed by you. Look at you. I want you to get your bags and go. Sort your life out. Do what you've got to do. But I don't want to see you doing it.'

The next two weeks were spent eating cheese sandwiches and getting into scrapes at local pubs, where he became a target. On one occasion, O'Sullivan fled after being attacked with pool cues.

O'Sullivan slid from No. 3 down to No. 16 in the world rankings during the 1995/96 season and remembered a chance meeting with a football legend as a turning point.

O'Sullivan was in Las Vegas for a boxing show where he bumped into Graeme Souness, who had been a hero in the Liverpool football team that conquered Europe in the 1980s.

Souness told him 'healthy body, healthy mind' and the message stuck with him.

Maria took him back and O'Sullivan discovered running.

'I had been out on a bender, I came home, went to the gym and a geezer said: "I'm going for a run, you want to come?"' he remembered. 'He takes me on a run and it killed me. It was outdoors, it was fresh air. It gave me a rush I had never felt before. It helped me deal with the stress, pressure and frustrations of the game I love.'

He got his weight down to 12 stones (76kg) and focused on his snooker career again.

'I HAD the best seat for one of the greatest moments in my sport,' said Mick Price.

'But people do take the piss sometimes. They shout "147" at me when I'm down the pub!'

Price was on the receiving end of 320 seconds of O'Sullivan at his very best. They played each other in the first round of the 1997 World Championship and Price was 8-5 down going into the final session.

'We were standing behind the curtain and were told we had to wait to go live on the BBC,' remembered Price.

'Playing at the Crucible was nerve-wracking enough anyway – and I really didn't need to hear that.'

Perhaps that wait was to blame for what Price described as 'a very poor safety shot' early in the 14th frame.

Five minutes 20 seconds later, O'Sullivan had completed the quickest maximum 147 break ever recorded ...

James Wattana previously held the record for the fastest televised 147, taking just seven minutes and nine seconds to make a maximum at the 1992 British Open and O'Sullivan shaved one minute, 49 seconds off that ...

'If I had stopped to think I would have missed,' O'Sullivan explained when asked about the speed of his clearance.

'I knew it was on after about four reds,' said Price, 'and I really wanted him to do it.'

After his seventh black, O'Sullivan swerved the cue ball into the reds and they broke perfectly for him to keep picking them off and stay on the black.

He left an angle on his 12th black that allowed him to separate the last two reds that were stuck together near the pink spot and moments later, the crowd were willing the cue ball around the angles and towards the yellow after the 15th black had been tucked away.

They cheered, clapped and whistled their approval when it stopped, perfectly placed, for O'Sullivan to snick in the yellow and as the finishing line approached, he accelerated.

He celebrated by tossing his chalk into the crowd and then asked for a replacement.

Price has made 28 maximums in practice himself. 'I've only ever had one made against me,' he said, 'but at least nobody saw it!'

O'Sullivan collected £147,000 for the maximum and £18,000 for the highest break of the championship, meaning he earned £515.62 per second or £30,937.69 per minute.

THE GOOD times didn't last.

O'Sullivan was stripped of the Irish Masters title in 1998 after testing positive for marijuana.

He put that down to having a piece of puff cake at a party, but the problem was deeper than that.

'I remember getting to every World Championship thinking: "I can't wait 'til this tournament is over 'cos then there's no more drugs tests, I can go out and smash it,"' wrote O'Sullivan.

'I loved a joint. The only problem with a joint is that one spliff follows another and another. [I would have] Any old drink, it didn't matter. Throw in a few spliffs. Then at 7am the sun would come up and I'd think: "I've done it again." The birds would be singing and I'd think: "I'm bang in trouble."

'At my worst I had to have a joint first thing in the morning, just to function.

'But loads of times snooker got in the way of my benders, rather than the other way round.'

O'Sullivan was pulled over by the police while driving in Stratford, east London, in June 2000 and it was noted that his 'eyes were bloodshot and glazed. He seemed agitated and his breath smelled strong'.

He was charged with refusing to provide a breath, blood or urine sample – he was later acquitted – but there was a problem.

O'Sullivan rang the National Drugs Helpline and was persuaded to spend four weeks at The Priory in Roehampton in south-west London.

O'Sullivan found comfort in being somewhere where 'nobody had any expectations of me' and when he heard the others' stories, he felt a connection.

O'Sullivan would describe his depression as 'illogical'. He had no reason to be unhappy – he knew he was more fortunate than so many others – but he was very unhappy.

At The Priory, he met others who knew how he felt and he wrote that after four weeks there, 'I loved myself.'

He returned to snooker at the Champions Cup in Brighton where he gave the press insights into his new mindset, saying: 'I'm much happier because I've realised snooker's not everything to me ... I heard Steve Davis say that this is a big season for me. It isn't. I'm just determined to enjoy myself and not have any expectations ... If I over-practice, it spoils my enjoyment of life off the table and of snooker itself. That's a trap I won't be falling into again.'

O'Sullivan won the Champions Cup, one of six trophies he lifted in the 2000/01 season.

'I had to get my life in order,' he said afterwards. 'Life is more than green baize and a bit of wood.'

O'Sullivan would later admit: 'I got a bit obsessed with it [snooker]. I couldn't get the perfectionism I wanted. I was a nightmare to be around so I spent a lot of time on my own because I didn't want to socialise with people. I became so driven to succeed and it done my head in.

I knew what I was capable of, but I wasn't achieving it. I was seeing other people getting results and I would be thinking: "I should be blowing them away."

'I don't think I suffered with depression, I'm not a depressed type of person, I think I suffered with snooker depression. I can go out and play, but take me out of there, I couldn't do life, I couldn't do people. I couldn't socialise. It was a nightmare.'

O'Sullivan faced familiar anguish ahead of the 2001 World Championship and was prescribed Prozac by a doctor a few days before he headed to Sheffield.

'Everyone was saying, "He's guaranteed to win it,"' he remembered, 'but I was suffering. I was down the doctor's a week before. I didn't want to be around people.

'I went to Sheffield and I was in my room and they asked me to do a radio interview. I thought: "How am I going to get through this?" I was blabbering, thinking: "What am I saying?" It was live and I said: "I'm not feeling too good. I'm suffering. I don't want to be here. I'm struggling." I felt I was going insane. I phoned the Samaritans.

'I knew if I stopped snooker a lot of my demons would have gone. But I couldn't walk away because my dad said, "Every time I see you play on the telly, it's like a visit" – so I had to play. He had ten years to go, so I had to play for another ten years. I had to do the right thing for someone else.'

O'Sullivan knew what was expected of him – and what he expected of himself.

He had watched Jimmy White fail to fulfil his potential, to the disappointment of millions.

White reached six World Championship finals – and lost them all. Four times, Stephen Hendry beat him, but really, it should have been White lifting the trophy in 1992.

He led 14-8 in the best-of-35-frames final and remembered: 'I'm in my corner thinking, "I will thank him, he helped me, I won't thank him." You lose focus.'

There was still a match to be won and, once White forgot that, Hendry pounced.

The Scot reeled off ten straight frames to break White's heart and there was more agony against Hendry two years later when White missed a black off its spot in the 35th and deciding frame.

These thoughts went through O'Sullivan's overactive mind during the 31st frame of the 2001 World Championship Final, against John Higgins.

O'Sullivan ought to have won the match by then and had time to imagine White's agony as Higgins got back to 17-14 and then watched the Scot put together a break of 45 in the next.

The refocused O'Sullivan stepped in after Higgins broke down on 45 to compile a match-winning break of 80.

'It was a massive monkey off my back,' said O'Sullivan of winning the World Championship at the ninth attempt, but as ever with him, the joy was tinged with sadness.

In quiet moments, the 25-year-old world champion wished he still enjoyed snooker as much as he did when he was a carefree ten-year-old.

SNOOKER MADE Ronnie O'Sullivan happy and it also made him sad. Sometimes, it bored him.

There were times when he seemed barely interested in matches he was playing in. When not at the table, O'Sullivan would wriggle uncomfortably in his chair, look into the crowd, chew his nails or play with his shoelaces.

He admitted once that he found matches that went beyond the best of 11 frames 'boring' and was spotted taking what he described as 'a power nap' during matches.

He was always likely to lose focus during his semi-final against Mark Selby at the 2007 UK Championship in Telford.

The final frame of Selby's quarter-final against Marco Fu had lasted a record-breaking 77 minutes, four minutes longer than the 27th frame of the 2006 World Championship Final between Peter Ebdon and Graeme Dott that had previously been the lengthiest frame in a televised tournament.

During that give-and-take tussle with Selby, O'Sullivan kept himself occupied when his opponent was at the table by looking at a spoon and counting the little dots that ran along its edge. When he lost count, he would start all over again.

Ronnie had to put down the spoon and pick up his cue in the 17th and final frame after Selby went for a long make-or-break red and missed. The red ran over the opposite corner pocket and O'Sullivan took his chance to post a maximum 147 break that took him through to the final.

'The spoon did it. I'd like to thank the spoon,' O'Sullivan said afterwards and he went on to beat Stephen Maguire 10-2 in the final.

On other occasions, O'Sullivan appeared to pick fights with rivals to motivate himself.

That was surely the only possible explanation for his comments ahead of his 2002 World Championship semi-final against Stephen Hendry.

Despite his dominance of the 1990s when he won seven world titles, Hendry didn't appear to have an enemy in the sport, until O'Sullivan revealed he had 'not a lot of respect' for the Scot.

He explained: 'I played him in the semi-finals a couple of years ago and we had this miss rule.

'You know when a certain player has made a genuine attempt and a miss was called against me.

'I really thought a lot of Stephen until he had that ball put back and he really went down in my estimations after that.

'There is not a lot of respect there at all.

'The most satisfying thing for me would be to send him home to Scotland as quickly as possible for a nice summer off.

'I'll say hello to him because it's hard to ignore someone, but he's not my cup of tea.

'He could do a moonie in front of me and I'd just say: "Get back to your sad little life."'

Hendry didn't bite and won the match 17-13.

O'Sullivan didn't seem devastated by defeat, rather he seemed exhilarated by the atmosphere the match had been played in.

Hendry said afterwards: 'Ronnie has been in The Priory being treated for depression. Why would I want his life?'

Mark Williams, his fellow graduate from the Class of '92, also became a target.

O'Sullivan wrote of Williams in his autobiography: 'I can't think of anyone in the game who likes him. He rubs everyone up the wrong way.'

The passage was brought to Williams's attention after being serialised in a daily tabloid newspaper and he shrugged: 'If you're an arsehole, you say stupid things.'

O'Sullivan responded: 'Mark should be thankful that he's mentioned in my book. Nobody will be writing books about him because he's not interesting.

'When you're great, people want to know about you, but he's just normal.

'I couldn't care less if he never said hello to me again because I'm a champion in my own life. I've come through a lot of trials and tribulations and I'm a survivor. And I'm sure I'll survive if Mark never speaks to me again.'

Williams won the 2003 World Championship, after O'Sullivan made a first-round exit. He was beaten 10-6 by Marco Fu, despite making a maximum 147.

O'SULLIVAN AND Peter Ebdon were never going to get on. O'Sullivan was emotional and impulsive; Ebdon intense and methodical.

O'Sullivan sometimes gave the impression that, win or lose, as long as he enjoyed playing and the crowd were entertained, he was happy, while Ebdon was a steely, win-at-all-costs competitor who played snooker purely for himself.

During their quarter-final at the 2005 World Championship, Ebdon took almost as long over a break of 12 as it had taken O'Sullivan to rattle in his record-breaking maximum eight years earlier.

That didn't make Ebdon the most popular player with the snooker public and his opponents weren't always impressed by the clenched-fist reaction to winning crucial frames.

Ebdon did things his way and in 2002 it took him all the way to the World Championship. He edged out Stephen Hendry in a 35th-frame decider, reversing a loss to the Scot in the final six years previously.

His interest in the 2005 World Championship looked likely to be ended by O'Sullivan after he fell 8-2 behind in their best-of-25-frames quarter-final.

Never rushed anyway, Ebdon applied the brakes. There was that break of 12 that took all of five minutes to compile and he spent another one minute, 40 seconds deliberating what appeared to be a straightforward enough safety shot.

O'Sullivan was known for being fidgety and restless and as Ebdon pondered every shot, he feigned sleep, asked a spectator the time and even grinned in Ebdon's face in an 'I-know-what-you're-up-to' manner when he came to the table.

The press and John Parrott in the BBC commentary box were unhappy with Ebdon after he went through 13-11.

Matthew Syed used the word 'cheating' in his report for *The Times* and that led to Ebdon suing the newspaper, unsuccessfully. O'Sullivan was never a bad loser.

'Peter's got to do what he's got to do,' he said. 'He's got a wife and four kids, so I can't criticise him. He's there to stop me playing.'

The next time they played in front of the cameras was at the Masters in 2006 and the match included possibly the longest frame of O'Sullivan's career.

It lasted 59 minutes.

After 44 minutes, O'Sullivan said he had to answer a call of nature – and Ebdon was left waiting seven minutes for him to return.

O'Sullivan ran out a 6-2 winner.

IF HE wasn't quarrelling with opponents or himself, O'Sullivan still had the snooker authorities to pick a fight with.

One of his grievances was the lack of prize money ...

O'Sullivan faced Mark King in the third round of the 2010 World Open in Glasgow and after sinking a red and black at the start of the third frame, he looked at how the balls were spread and stopped to ask referee Jan Verhaas if there was a money prize for a maximum.

BY THE time he was told there was no prize on offer, other than the £4,000 for the tournament's highest break, O'Sullivan had reached 48 and he went on to take blacks with all 15 reds before sinking yellow, green, brown, blue, pink and ... that was it.

Ronnie just had to knock in the black off its spot to complete the maximum, but, upset there was no prize money for the feat, he shook King's hand to signal the break was over and it took a word from the referee to persuade him to complete the maximum that wrapped up a 3-0 win.

Explaining himself, O'Sullivan told reporters: 'What's the point of making a 147 if you're only going to make £4,000?

'But the ref played a guilt trip on me and said: "Come on, do it for your fans."

'And I thought, "OK, because I haven't got long to play anyway, so I might as well go out on a high." But I wasn't going to pot it because four grand, once you've paid the taxes...'

O'Sullivan received a huge boost weeks later when his father was released from prison and O'Sullivan Sr was in Llandudno to see his son win the Premier League for the sixth time in seven years.

O'Sullivan's melancholy was hard to shrug off permanently and, in an attempt to clear his mind, he went to work as a farm labourer, withdrawing from all competitions after winning a fourth world title in 2012.

He told the press: 'The farm has got sheep, pigs, cows, goats, chickens, horses – and I've been getting the green wellies on.

'I've been cleaning out stables and pig sties, taking down fences, putting rubbish into barrels and clearing mud. It has been mainly manual work, also getting big bales of hay in to feed the animals.

'I was getting so bored I had to do something and needed a goal to get out of bed in the morning. I didn't want stress, as that was what made me pull out of snooker, so I decided to go and do something unpaid.

'I get there about 8am, do my three- or four-mile run first because it is right in the forest, then come back and do about six hours' work.

'There are personal things I need to sort out before I can even think of a return [to snooker].'

O'Sullivan said there was a chance he may not return to defend his World Championship in 2013, but with the deadline for entry only days away, he entered and somehow, went on to lift the trophy for the fifth time without losing a single session.

Stuart Bingham, thumped 13-4 in the quarter-finals, described O'Sullivan as 'unbelievable', but as ever, Ronnie was less satisfied.

After making six centuries to see off Barry Hawkins 18-12 in the final, the joy of pulling off 'one of the most amazing things I've ever done' was mixed with melancholy.

'I've probably not got that many years left,' said O'Sullivan and further proof of his mental unrest came when he got into trouble at the German Masters in Barnsley for no other reason than he felt like getting into trouble.

He crashed out to Thepchaiya Un-Nooh, the 2008 world amateur champion from Thailand, and was later fined £1,000 for refusing to tuck his shirt in and abusing the head referee after he was asked again.

He went on to upset the WPBSA with claims made in his second autobiography, regarding his World Championship Final victory over Hawkins.

O'Sullivan said the cloth had been changed ahead of the final 'to stop me winning it'.

He claimed the new cloth was slower and heavier and therefore suited Hawkins's more dogged approach.

Nonetheless, O'Sullivan went on to make six century breaks during the match, but wrote: 'I know the minute I'm not doing well, or the minute they think snooker fans have given up on me, they'll get rid of me.'

RONNIE O'SULLIVAN knew what people said about him.

'The media make out I've won this tournament before I even turn up and that can be difficult in such an intense environment,' he said ahead of the 2016 World Championship.

For the purposes of a television documentary, Steve Davis was filmed driving O'Sullivan to the Crucible.

Davis fought back tears as he thought of all his memorable nights there, while O'Sullivan shuffled uncomfortably in his seat.

The words he muttered when thinking of the World Championship were 'grind' and 'anxiety'.

O'Sullivan had found some answers after being introduced to Dr Steve Peters.

Peters had worked with the Great Britain cycling team ahead of the 2012 London Olympics and O'Sullivan described his role as helping him 'find a way not to beat myself up and ask: "What's the point?"'

The partnership worked.

O'Sullivan said after winning the 2013 World Championship: 'Going to see Steve is probably the best thing I've done in my life. He's helped me deal with difficult emotions that were holding me back. He's helped me turn my life around.'

Peters would say the 'fear of failure' had paralysed O'Sullivan, who explained how badly he took losses.

He said: 'I can play and not feel my self-worth depends on winning.'

O'Sullivan's self-esteem was boosted when he was named in the 2016 New Year's Honours List and he won the first televised tournament of the year after Peters came to his rescue ahead of the Masters.

During the tournament, O'Sullivan's demons returned. He talked of being 'petrified' and said he was suffering with insomnia.

Peters made the trip to London to talk to O'Sullivan and after he had thrashed Hawkins 10-1, Ronnie said: 'I owe Steve for this one.

'I was able to contain my emotions and not think about the importance of the match.'

O'SULLIVAN FOUND a way to relieve the boredom of post-match interviews. He would have fun.

On one occasion, he would only answer that his waistcoat was too tight and he left reporters bemused at another when he started singing Oasis's worldwide hit 'Wonderwall'.

O'Sullivan also adopted a bizarre Australian accent during the 2019 Players Championship in Preston. He explained: 'The Aussies are just winners, you've got to love a winner.

'Our English, we love a loser, so I thought I'm fed up of being a loser, so I'm going to talk like a winner, like the Aussies.'

He claimed the final, against Neil Robertson, was an all-Australian affair.

Robertson was from Melbourne, while O'Sullivan called Essex home ...

For a few years, O'Sullivan had talked of wanting to reach the milestone of 1,000 century breaks.

He went into the final on 997 and made two more on the way to opening up a 9-4 lead in the best-of-19-frames duel.

O'Sullivan broke in the 14th frame and forced an error from Robertson.

The Australian was unable to find the top cushion with a safety shot and O'Sullivan picked out a red to the middle pocket that set him on his way.

He raced to his half-century and after that, every shot he played was clapped and cheered by the audience.

O'Sullivan allowed himself a smile after reaching 91 before a red and black took him to the brink.

O'Sullivan savoured the moment. He got down to play the shot right-handed – and had a rethink.

He switched to play left-handed and rolled the red into the corner pocket to reach his landmark.

He raised his finger to acknowledge the crowd's cheers and many of them stayed on their feet as a smiling O'Sullivan set about clearing the table.

The break reached 134 before O'Sullivan went in off the final black.

Later that month, he equalled Hendry's record of 36 ranking titles by winning the Tour Championship, a victory that took him to No. 1 in the world rankings for the first time since 2010.

O'Sullivan went past Hendry in the best way possible, by capturing his sixth World Championship in August 2020, and at 44 years and 254 days, he also became the oldest world champion since Ray Reardon in 1978.

POSSIBLY THE most shocking story ever written about O'Sullivan appeared in the pages of the tabloid press in February 2021.

Fiancée Laila Rouass revealed that O'Sullivan was now boring!

The actress said as part of her wellbeing studies, she researched the lessons of Buddha and Greek philosophers.

She said O'Sullivan had listened to these teachings and become calmer. He preferred watching television and going out to dinner over partying.

Those days, Laila said, were 'well and truly over'.

The new lifestyle appeared to suit O'Sullivan. He equalled Hendry's record of seven world titles by winning the 2022 championship and celebrated with his father and two of his children.

O'Sullivan was unable to add an eighth title 12 months later, but by then he had accepted there was more to life than winning snooker matches.

'If you'd asked me in 1998 or 1999 where I'd be in 24, 25 years, I'd never have said: "Winning the World Championship, feeling good, come through whatever you've come through,"' he said before bowing out in the quarter-finals to Luca Brecel.

'I've made it to 47, not in some nuthouse or a drug den, looking for my next fix.

'I'm an addict. I know that. I channel it into running or the gym. So when people go, "Why is he in the gym?" Mate, that gym could have been a crack house. I just choose to go to the gym.

'I choose to do everything that keeps me away from pubs, drinking, partying.

'My mate once said, "If you stay outside a barbers' long enough, you'll end up getting a haircut." I need to be near gyms, running clubs, running people.

'My wellbeing is good. That's rule No. 1. Rule No. 2 is to remember rule No. 1 – and there is no rule No. 3.'

FIGHTS AND FIXES

RUMOUR HAS it that after the police pulled him over on suspicion of drink-driving, Quinten Hann asked: 'Don't you know who I am?'

He was a pin-up, fighter, cheat and on his day, one of the best snooker players in the world, if not the most popular.

'A lot of the other players don't like Quinten,' said O'Sullivan, 'because although they pot all the balls, he pulls the birds.'

There had been a time when Hann looked a better prospect than O'Sullivan.

They were teenagers when they first came across each other, at the World Masters in Birmingham in January 1991, when both were entered in the junior event.

O'Sullivan bowed out in the quarter-finals, beaten 5-4 by John Higgins, while Hann lost to Mark Williams in the semi-finals. During the tournament, Hann went into the record books when, at 13 years old, he became the youngest player to make a televised century.

There was another side to the Australian teenager and later that year, the Australian Billiards and Snooker Council handed him a suspended ban for spitting on a rival's mother. The council dismissed Hann's claim that he was engaged in a spitting competition with a friend and the woman had the misfortune to get in the way.

The ban was implemented after Hann swore at a referee during the New South Wales Junior Championship in January 1993.

Hann had served his apprenticeship around the Australian pool halls.

'When I was just ten years old, I was playing pool almost every weekend and making about $25 a day by laying down challenges to opponents,' he remembered. 'I was taking the pubs by storm, but by mum was getting worried about me hanging out in sleazy places and contacted a number out of the paper for a snooker teacher.'

The lessons worked and after his mother sold her car to fund his trip to England, Hann turned professional in 1995. He was soon snapped up by a modelling agency, but Hann was more than just a pretty face.

In 1998, he qualified for the World Championship, the first Australian to do so for six years. He was beaten 10-9 by Mark Williams and went on to play O'Sullivan in the last 32 of the 2000 Grand Prix in Telford, a match that raised questions about Hann's temperament.

Twice, Hann broke off by smashing into the reds off the side and bottom cushions, a move better suited to pool.

And on two occasions when O'Sullivan broke, Hann responded by ploughing the cue ball into the pack of reds with his first shot.

He would later explain he fancied he had a 50-50 chance of potting a red off the break by smashing into the pack, but it didn't work. O'Sullivan whitewashed him 5-0 and sections of the crowd booed Hann afterwards. The WPBSA later fined him £750 for 'unprofessional behaviour'.

Hann gave O'Sullivan a better match in the quarter-finals of the UK Championship in Bournemouth later that year.

He played in his socks after breaking a bone in a foot during a parachute accident and opened up a shock 4-2 lead, but O'Sullivan turned the match his way with a dazzling three-frame burst where he outscored Hann 279-0.

The conclusion of every television pundit watching was that Hann was an underachiever, a player who with more desire could be ranked in the top eight. That claim put a smile on his face and O'Sullivan's when it was put to him in the post-match interview.

'They make it sound easy, don't they?' said O'Sullivan, while Hann explained that it was hard being a snooker player from Australia.

The professional circuit was played around Europe, mostly Britain, and Hann would reveal in other interviews that he had the same sort of relationship with snooker that O'Sullivan had.

Hann said he resented the sport because 'it was the reason I was away from home'.

Perhaps that resentment was part of the reason why he turned up for the 2000 World Championship qualifiers in Newport wearing combat trousers. Told, as he knew he would be, he had to wear smarter trousers, Hann went to a local shop and bought a pair.

He played with the labels still attached and once the match was over, Hann returned his trousers to the shop.

Then there were his crazy breaks.

He drove the cue ball straight into the reds at the 2002 World Championship, against Paul Hunter and Stephen Lee.

Astonishingly, he potted a red into the middle pocket against Lee with the opening shot of the seventh frame and took a bow as the crowd cheered. Hann missed his next shot, a black into the middle pocket, and went on to lose 13-3.

What was he thinking? David Hendon, the knowledgeable snooker commentator and writer, argued that Hann 'needed to give himself an excuse to lose. If he gave the match away he could rationalise it in his own mind that he hadn't really been beaten'.

Hann could always tell himself that he could have won the match, if he had been bothered. Whatever he was thinking, Hann didn't appear to have the temperament required to be a top player.

He reached the semi-finals of the Irish Masters in 2004 – his best run in a ranking tournament – and then conceded the seventh frame against Peter Ebdon when there were still six reds left on the table out of sheer frustration after missing the black off its spot.

At the World Championship a few weeks later, Hann had to be separated from Andy Hicks by referee Lawrie Allandale during their first-round match after Hann challenged him to a fight, saying: 'You are short and bald and you can have me outside whenever you want.'

The following day, Hann was apologetic, saying: 'I'm not proud of what I said. I feel bad about it, but everyone wants to win so badly at the Crucible. I haven't got the best temper in the world and I was out of order.'

Hicks, nicknamed 'The Cream of Devon', was a 10-4 winner and played O'Sullivan next.

Again, there was friction.

In the third frame, Hicks was on a break of 40 when O'Sullivan got up from his seat and picked up a red to indicate he had conceded.

In the next frame, Hicks walked out while O'Sullivan was at the table.

O'Sullivan went on to win the grudge match 13-11 and though Hann said he regretted threatening Hicks, he still ended up boxing a fellow professional snooker player in a bout amusingly titled 'Pot Thwack'.

Mark King, who also happened to be bald, said there was bad feeling between them ever since he took £500 off Hann following a match at a club when the Australian was only 16 years old.

Both joined amateur boxing clubs and the bout went ahead at the York Hall in Bethnal Green, a famous venue for boxing in London's East End.

O'Sullivan was in Hann's corner and despite King being considered a marginal favourite going into the three-round bout, Hann ran out a points winner.

'The bad feeling between us was partly to hype up the fight,' he said afterwards, 'but we've certainly never really been mates.

'I don't like most of the other snooker players. They're not my sort of people.'

HANN'S FIRST-ROUND match against Marcus Campbell at the 2004 Grand Prix looked like a comfortable win for the Australian. He was ranked 18th in the world, 45 places above Campbell, who was without a win on the circuit for almost a year. The rumour was, Hann, perhaps expecting a straightforward victory, hadn't been practising and had other things on his mind.

Whatever the reason, Campbell was a 5-3 winner, a result that gave several punters who had backed the Scot a good payout. The WPBSA didn't see anything suspicious in the match, but *The Sun* sniffed a possible story.

Tipped off that Hann may throw matches for money, two reporters, posing as businessmen, arranged to meet him at his chalet at Pontin's, Prestatyn, where the World Championship qualifiers were being held.

Hann told the undercover reporters that losing to Ken Doherty at the forthcoming China Open 'could be a money-spinner' and was also quoted as saying: 'Listen, you want me to lose 5-0? I'll lose 10-0. I don't care. I'm a businessman. I just want to make money.'

Hann said of his loss to Campbell: 'I know a few people had big bets on Campbell and they collected £40,000 odd. Betting was suspended and they watched the match, but it was all sweet.'

He was offered £5,000 up front followed by £45,000 if he lost 5-0 to Doherty, but Hann asked for a downpayment of £20,000 that was rejected.

Hann seemed keen to maintain the relationship, telling the reporters: 'Give me a call in September.'

The story was printed only days after Hann was acquitted of two charges of sexual assault, against a singer and an actress, who claimed he behaved like 'a crazed animal' and left them fearing for their lives.

The match-fixing allegations would be harder to escape, though Hann's mother, Amanda, offered an explanation.

She said when contacted by reporters: 'I've been on the phone to him three or four times today.

'Of course he's not worried about the story. He thinks it's absolutely hilarious. All I say is, "Bring on the charges, bring on the court case."

'Quinten knew he was a journalist and that is why he didn't take the money.

'He thought it was amusing this fellow was trying to hand him [the money] and he didn't fall for that bait. It's his career, his living, and he's not stupid.'

The evidence against Hann was overwhelming and he acknowledged as much, resigning his membership of the WPBSA before a hearing that concluded he 'knowingly entered into an agreement to join in an unlawful enterprise to fix the results of certain snooker competitions in return for financial gain'.

He was banned for eight years and fined £10,000.

JOHN HIGGINS won the World Championship in 1998, 2007 and 2009.

His defence of the title in 2010 ended with a shock second-round defeat to 52-year-old Steve Davis, but much worse was to come for the world No. 1.

On the day of the final, between Neil Robertson and Graeme Dott, Sunday tabloid the *News of the World* 'revealed' they had footage of Higgins 'shaking hands on a disgraceful deal to fix a string of high-profile matches after demanding a £300,000 kickback'.

Higgins, it was claimed, had been the victim of a 'sting' by the newspaper and the claims were a huge blow to snooker's credibility.

Higgins was one of the sport's leading names, a graduate from the Class of '92 who Steve Davis would say was the most complete player in snooker history.

In 1994/95, Higgins, from Wishaw in Lanarkshire, Scotland, had become the first teenager to win three ranking events in a season, the Grand Prix, International Open and British Open, beating Class of '92 contemporary O'Sullivan in the final of the latter.

The World Championship followed in 1998 and on the way to lifting the trophy Higgins made 14 century breaks, a record subsequently broken by Stephen Hendry.

Higgins added further world titles in 2007 and 2009 before the *News of the World* story left his future in doubt.

Higgins and manager Pat Mooney had met one of their undercover reporters at a hotel in Kyiv in Ukraine and appeared to agree to 'throw' four frames in exchange for money.

Video footage on the newspaper's website showed Higgins jokingly asking if there were any hidden cameras and going on to apparently 'explain' how he could throw frames.

He said: 'If you keep leaving, leaving, leaving chances people are going to say: "What is happening here?"'

'But against other players, it is no problem.'

Higgins and Mooney were shown shaking hands with the 'businessman' and sharing a toast.

Barry Hearn, the chairman of the WPBSA, issued a statement within hours that read: 'John Higgins has been suspended from future WPBSA tournaments, pending an immediate inquiry.

'Pat Mooney has resigned from the WPBSA board and his resignation has been accepted with immediate effect.

'The WPBSA inquiry will be headed by David Douglas and will be carried out with the utmost urgency. This matter has brought the very fabric of the game into question.

'The strongest possible message needs to be sent out that any such behaviour has no part to play in our game and will not be tolerated. Wrongdoing will be severely dealt with.'

Though he stressed Higgins would be given the chance to clear his name, Hearn told BBC Sport he was enduring 'one of the most disappointing days I have had in 35 years dealing in professional sport'.

Higgins protested his innocence in a statement.

'In my 18 years as a professional snooker player I have never deliberately missed a shot, never mind intentionally lost a frame or match,' he stated.

'In all honestly, I became very worried at the way the conversation developed in Kyiv. When it was suggested that I throw frames for large sums of money I was really spooked and just wanted out of the hotel and on the plane home.

'I didn't know if this was the Russian Mafia or who we were dealing with at that stage. I felt the best course of action was just play along with these guys and get out of Russia.

'Those who know me are aware of my love for snooker and that I would never do anything to damage the integrity of the sport I love.

'My conscience is 100% clear.'

The story was especially unsettling for Dott on the eve of the World Championship Final because the Scot, world champion four years earlier, was also managed by Mooney.

Neil Robertson denied him another world title, beating him by an 18-13 scoreline.

THE INVESTIGATION into the Higgins match-fixing claims was held over two days and overseen by Sports Resolutions UK, an independent dispute resolution company.

David Douglas, a former high-ranking Metropolitan Police officer, led the inquiry, which included studying video footage and talking to all those involved.

Higgins denied 'agreeing or offering' to accept bribes and 'agreeing to engage in corrupt or fraudulent conduct', but admitted the lesser charge of bringing snooker into disrepute by not reporting the approach that was made.

In his defence, Higgins said he went into the meeting believing there was, in Douglas's words, 'a huge sponsorship deal on the table' and knew nothing of any frame-fixing plot.

Once the meeting got underway and Higgins understood the situation, he claimed he said whatever was necessary to escape.

Douglas went along with that, later saying: 'John was literally walking into that meeting when Mr Mooney said to him: "By the way, they might bring up throwing a few frames, just go along with it," or words to that effect.

'John was going in as a rabbit in the headlights.'

Higgins was still fined £75,000 and handed a six-month ban for bringing the game into disrepute.

Ian Mill QC said Higgins had been 'foolish' and that Mooney had 'committed the most egregious betrayal of trust'.

The hearing concluded that Mooney was aware at least three weeks before the meeting in Kyiv that the journalist posing as a businessman wanted to 'make money through gambling in circumstances where frames in snooker matches were deliberately thrown'.

Though the match-fixing charges were dropped, Mooney admitted bringing the game into disrepute by failing to disclose the approach and 'intentionally giving the impression to others that they were agreeing to act in breach of the betting rules'. He was suspended for life while Higgins was able to resume his career in a few weeks. The six-month ban was backdated to May, when he had originally been suspended.

SHAILESH 'JOE' JOGIA had ambitions to be snooker's new 'Mr Maximum'.

As a teenager, Jogia played at the Leicester snooker club owned by the original 'Mr Maximum', Willie Thorne.

Jogia and Thorne were similar in that they produced their best form on the practice table.

Jogia reckoned he had made 80 maximum breaks in practice, but in ranking events he never got beyond the last 32 and his highest ranking was No. 44.

He was due to make a rare appearance in front of the television cameras at the Snooker Shoot-Out in January 2012.

Traditionalists had scoffed at Barry Hearn's idea of matches lasting a maximum of ten minutes with players having only a few seconds to play each shot.

But, for all his millions, Hearn was still in touch with what the paying public wanted.

He knew there would be an audience for Snooker Shoot Out, in the same way there had been an audience for other sports played over shorter formats, such as Twenty20 cricket and boxing's equivalent, Prizefighter.

First held in 1990 as 'Shoot Out', the tournament was revived in 2011, and sell-out crowds in Blackpool were thrilled by drama, flukes – and controversy.

The £32,000 top prize was won by Nigel Bond, a less flamboyant 45-year-old from Derbyshire whose best days were thought to be more than a decade behind him.

The first-round match between Jimmy Michie and Marcus Campbell attracted unwanted interest as several bookmakers stopped taking bets after Campbell was heavily backed.

The WPBSA vowed to launch an investigation into a match that proved to be Michie's last as a professional.

He retired shortly after his defeat.

The following year, Jogia was investigated after bets were placed on him to lose his first-round match against Matthew Selt at the Snooker Shoot Out.

Jogia explained that because he had a knee injury, he would be unable to get around the table and presumably, punters had found out and bet against him.

He pulled out a day before the tournament began and it was subsequently discovered that in the space of five days in the week leading up to the match, 19 bets were placed in bookmakers in the Leicester area on Jogia to lose.

Fourteen bets totalled £4,830 and the rest were declined.

The WPBSA banned Jogia for two years and handed him a £2,000 fine to help pay toward the costs of the investigation. They issued a statement that revealed Jogia 'sent 33 text messages and made three calls to one of the persons placing the bets and 42 text messages and one call to the other.

'Joe has failed to provide a consistent or detailed explanation as to the reason for the contact.

'Initially, Joe Jogia claimed that the reason for the betting must be that people were aware of an injury that he had suffered, but four of the suspicious bets were placed before he claimed to have suffered the injury and a further seven of the bets were placed before he sought medical attention.'

Jogia didn't go quietly, telling newspaper reporters he had been made 'a scapegoat'.

'I've done nothing wrong,' he said. 'I didn't even play the match, it's shocking.

'With everything that's going on in snooker – the corruption – they couldn't take it out on the top boys because of where they are in the world. But I've done nothing wrong and all of a sudden they take it out on me. I've been made a scapegoat. I'm going to go and tell my stories now, about people on the tour and what they get up to.'

Though World Snooker said they 'strongly refuted' the claims made by Jogia, a few months later they suspended Stephen Lee as they investigated suspicious betting patterns and Jogia sold his stories to the *Sunday Mirror*.

He told the newspaper he first experienced corruption during a tournament in Sheffield in 2006.

'A few of us were having a few drinks and we were all due to play the next day,' said Jogia, 'and then one of them suggested, "Why don't we get our heads together and get £2,000 each?" I walked away. I didn't know the other results, but I certainly won that match.'

He recalled another occasion when he got talking to a former professional.

'We had a drink and he asked if I wanted to be part of the team,' said Jogia. 'When he said what it was about I couldn't believe it.

'He said he had 12 professional players and at any one time had a player who could throw a game. He mentioned one player's name and I was halfway out of the door.'

Jogia was also convinced that a former top-10 player 'threw' a match against him.

He said: 'He was hitting safety shots a bit thick, losing the cue ball and missing pots by a long way. It was getting quite bad ... it was embarrassing, like playing against Stevie Wonder.

'At the interval I went to the toilet when I was 3-1 in front. I smiled at him and said: "I take it you are not going to win this game." He just smiled at me and walked away. I went on to win.

'When you are a professional player you can tell when someone is making mistakes and playing like an amateur.

'You set yourself up for hard pots and eventually you are going to miss them. It would be a series of bad positional plays. One leads to another, making it hard to get on the next ball, so you wouldn't be making obvious silly mistakes.'

There was another incident, Jogia claimed, at the Players Tour Championship Event Four in Germany.

He said: 'I heard some players messing about in the next room. They were a bit sheepish when I walked in but they brought me into the conversation. There were three players and they said they would get £9,000 each for all three losing but if I came in it would work out to £15,000 each.

'They were trying to persuade me to do it for half an hour. They said if I got the train to London the following week and met one of the players he would hand over £15,000 in an envelope.'

The idea was to spread bets around various bookmakers online and on the high street to avoid suspicion.

Jogia said: 'I said "no" to them, left and won my game. I don't think it was a coincidence that all those three lost. I didn't approach the authorities. I just thought, "Leave it." I didn't want to get involved.'

THE WPBSA would uncover 'the worst case of corruption' a year later.

At the culmination of their investigation, Stephen Lee, who had been ranked as high as No. 5 around a decade earlier, was found guilty of match fixing in September 2013, and handed a 12-year ban. Lee had fixed seven matches during 2008 and 2009 – including his first-round match against Ryan Day at the 2009 World Championship.

The tribunal discovered that three groups of gamblers made nearly £100,000 betting on Lee's matches.

Lee had deliberately lost matches against Ken Doherty and Marco Fu at the 2008 Malta Cup and agreed to lose the first frame against both Stephen Hendry and Mark King at the 2008 UK Championship.

He also lost matches by a predetermined score to Neil Robertson at the 2008 Malta Cup and to Mark Selby at the 2009 China Open, as well as conspiring to lose to Day at the Crucible.

Tribunal chairman Adam Lewis QC described Lee as 'a weak man in a vulnerable position' brought about by financial problems rather than 'a cynical cheat', but still, he was handed the longest ban in snooker's history.

The WPBSA had sought a lifetime ban, but the organisation's head of disciplinary, former Metropolitan Police detective superintendent Nigel Mawer, insisted the 12-year suspension and an order to pay £40,000 costs was effectively the same.

'Hand on heart I believe it is a very, very clean sport,' he said. 'I have only had to investigate four incidents in 7,000 matches and two of those have led to suspensions, which puts it in context.'

Lee told Sky Sports News: 'I'm absolutely devastated.

'I've done nothing wrong. I'm totally innocent.

'My kids are getting picked on at school and it's totally outrageous, what I've been put through.

'I didn't have a lawyer to represent me. I believe if I'd had a lawyer in there it'd have been a different outcome completely.'

He claimed a newspaper interview would 'paint the full picture' and added: 'It's over, isn't it? My career's over.'

Hearn reacted by saying: 'The courts today don't seem to like to give out lifetime bans in any sport; this seems to be the policy generally.

'But 12 years out of the professional circuit, it's going to be a mountain to come back from that, I don't see any way back.

'We can never stop human nature, there'll always be temptation to take the easy road.

'But what they've got to do is understand the penalties and the punishments that are handed out if they err.'

O'Sullivan responded to the news with a Tweet that brought him as much attention as Lee.

He wrote: 'I've heard there's many more players who throw snooker matches. I suppose Steve Lee just got caught out.

'No need to worry if you've got nothing to hide, but plenty of people have got loads to hide. That's why there is no free speech. They don't like you doing that. They like to keep things under the carpet.'

By 'they', O'Sullivan presumably meant the WPBSA and chairman Jason Ferguson responded by saying the Lee case was proof that match fixing wasn't kept 'under the carpet'.

Forced to backtrack, O'Sullivan said that when he wrote on Twitter he was referring to 'rumours of many years ago when there were only a few tournaments on the circuit' and added snooker 'has undoubtedly been cleaned up since World Snooker has been taken over by Barry Hearn'.

JIMMY BROWN AND THE REST OF THE CAST

IN 1998, the unthinkable happened.

Jimmy White became part of the establishment when he was awarded an MBE for services to snooker in the New Year's Honours List – or should that be Jimmy Brown?

The government's decision to ban tobacco sponsorship of sporting events in 2003 was a blow to snooker, though the World Championship was exempt until 2006.

There had been a decline in tobacco sponsorship over the previous decade or so, but still, the new law left the Scottish and Welsh Opens looking for a replacement sponsor.

Upon hearing that HP Sauce were going to sponsor the brown ball at tournaments, White had an idea and ahead of the 2005 Masters, he announced he had changed his name to 'James Brown' by deed poll.

The BBC insisted it would still call him 'Jimmy White' throughout the tournament.

Because advertising was banned by the BBC, they felt HP Sauce would be able to gain some publicity were 'White' to be known as 'Brown'.

White threatened legal action in a letter sent to the BBC.

It read: 'As you may well be aware from some of the media coverage over the past week, I have officially changed my name by deed poll to James Brown.

'I am writing to you to inform you of this and more importantly to ensure that in any references to me made during your broadcast of the Masters, be they verbal or visual or in captions, you always refer to me in the context of my new identity.

'As has always been the case, I am happy for Jimmy to be used instead of the more formal James. Therefore please refer to me as Jimmy Brown in all instances for the duration of the tournament.'

The BBC answered that he had entered the tournament as 'Jimmy White' rather than 'Jimmy Brown' and concluded: 'We will refer to Jimmy White in our editorial coverage as that's how he's known to millions of viewers.'

World Snooker backed the BBC in a statement.

'He is referred to as Jimmy White in the event's promotional literature. He will be announced into the arena by that name and will be called Jimmy White by referees and television commentators.

'The name Jimmy Brown will only be used in relation to his promotional activities with HP Sauce, sponsors of the brown ball during the tournament.'

As Jimmy White, he reached the semi-finals where O'Sullivan thumped him 6-1.

O'Sullivan was awarded an OBE in 2016, much to his surprise.

Three years earlier he had said on the subject of honours: 'It would be a disgrace to give it to someone like me. I'm just not that type of guy, am I?

'As long as I am loved by my fans and my public, and when I die people might still have a look on YouTube and say, "This guy played the game better than anyone who ever played," then for me that is better than anything.'

O'Sullivan grew a moustache in 2020, his tribute to a former star who had fallen on hard times.

Willie Thorne died in a Spanish hospital aged 66 after a battle with leukaemia and sepsis.

O'Sullivan called Thorne 'a beautiful man', Hendry called him 'one of the funniest men I've ever met' and the *Sunday Mirror* described him as 'a rarity', explaining: 'Thorne wasn't just nice when the cameras were on him. He just was a nice man.' The new games room in The Phoenix Club needed a name in 2002.

The Jocky Wilson Suite, named after the 1982 world darts champion, had burned down and once the room had been rebuilt, it was decided it should be renamed.

Brian Potter, owner of The Phoenix Club, toyed with the idea of calling it The Steven Redgrave Suite after the Olympic rowing champion, but instead he went for Tony Knowles.

The reasoning was, Knowles was a local lad and 'The Tony Knowles Suite' chimed with Potter's rather offbeat way of looking at the world.

This all happened in the imagination of comedian Peter Kay, who wrote and starred in cult situation comedy *Phoenix Nights*.

There was a framed poster of Knowles on the wall and after hearing about the 'honour', Knowles turned up on set during filming.

He handed Kay a poster from his own collection, but the hoped for cameo appearance didn't materialise.

Knowles kept playing snooker and at 65, he entered Q School, hoping to regain his place on the World Snooker Tour after an absence of 22 years!

Quinten Hann got in more trouble after leaving snooker behind, cheating clients out of millions after setting up a financial company which dealt with foreign exchange trading.

Hann, calling himself James Sonny Quinten Hunter, set up a company called Monarch FX that was investigated in 2014.

He told clients they would receive a 5% monthly return on investments if they forked out at least $15,000 to receive automated cutting-edge advice based on complex computer algorithms.

Clients typically lost 40–50% of their investments, the courts discovered.

Hann was banned from the financial services industry for four years, while former clients of Monarch FX were left chasing compensation for their losses.

BIBLIOGRAPHY

Burn, Gordon, *Pocket Money* (Faber & Faber, 1986)

Davis, Steve, *Steve Davis Snooker Champion: His Own Story* (Arthur Barker Ltd, 1981)

Everton, Clive, *Guinness Book of Snooker* (Superlatives Ltd, 1981)

Everton, Clive, *The Story of Billiards and Snooker* (Cassell, 1979)

McGinley, Gareth, *Heart Breaks: The Tony Knowles Story* (Short Run Press, 2019)

Morrison, Ian, *The Hamlyn Encyclopedia of Snooker* (Hamlyn, 1985)

Rafferty, Jean, *The Cruel Game: The Inside Story of Snooker* (Elm Tree Books, 1983)

Reardon, Ray, *Classic Snooker* (David & Charles, 1976)

Reardon, Ray with Hennessey, John, *Enjoying Snooker with Ray Reardon: A personal guide to the game* (St Michael, 1985)

Smith, Terry, *Snooker: The Players, the Shots, the Matches* (St Michael, 1989) Virgo, John, *Let Me Tell You About Alex: Crazy Days and Nights on the Road with 'The Hurricane'* (John Blake, 2011)

Williams, Luke and Gadsby, Paul, *Masters of the Baize* (Mainstream Publishing, 2005)